REVERSING GENOCIDE

The Moral Philosophy of Freedom

Volume One

The Healing Balm

Copyright © 2018 by The Healing Balm

All rights reserved. No part of this publication may be reproduced, distributed, or transmitted in any form or by any means, including photocopying, recording, or other electronic or mechanical methods, without the prior written permission of the publisher, except in the case of brief quotations embodied in critical reviews and certain other noncommercial uses permitted by copyright law.

Cover Illustration by Tanisha Benjamin

ISBN: 978-1-7326934-7-0

Liberation's Publishing LLC
West Point, Mississippi
www.liberationspublishing.com

Reversing Genocide

The Moral Philosophy of Freedom

Volume One

The Healing Balm

Acknowledgments

Due to the nature of the beast who dominates the globe with merciless violence, it is probably wise for us to skip the acknowledgement of specific individuals. The forces of constant terror, murder, and harassment could use the acknowledgements of this book to penalize people for their association with the exposure of truth and reality written in the following pages. The destroyers of freedom tend to be hyper-aggressive towards people who can see through their deception. For example, recently one of the Move 9 was released from prison after 40 years. The shootout in Philadelphia in 1978 left one police officer dead. Nine people in the house were charged for the murder, because of association, even though the police officer may have been killed in crossfire by his own fellow slave enforcement fraternity. The sister released from prison fired no rounds because she had no weapon. But because of association and relentless injustice, she was still sentenced from 30 years to life in prison. For this reason, we will not list specific acknowledgements. We do not wish harm to anybody. We just want to be free. Please keep this in mind as you read on.

With that said, however, we would like to generally acknowledge all those individuals and groups who bravely stand unaligned with the destroyers of the Earth. We acknowledge those who have learned to think in terms of sustainability. This is a necessary mindset for overcoming domination and destruction. Sustainability will enable peace and longevity. To the contrary, Euro-Jewish global domination is not sustainable. War is not sustainable. Male dominant culture that produces war is also not sustainable. Oppositely, we have to love, support, and acknowledge women in order to develop a caring paradigm. So, we acknowledge the feminine energy that provides balance toward a harmonious social order. We acknowledge the freedom fighters who have not allowed freedom to be defined by slavers and private banks. We acknowledge those who take a strong stand for human autonomy and defend indigenous people against aggression. We acknowledge the natural and societal forces that are bringing the power of humanity back to the people.

Table of Contents

Introduction 9
Chapter 1 Interpretations of Freedom 19
Chapter 2 Marching and Dreaming 59
    Essay: March Madness 59
    Short Story: Freedom's family 78
    Speech: Waking Up from the Dream 82
Chapter 3 Human Rights 123
References 205
    Books: 205
    Videos: 208
    Websites: 209

"In a context of universal deceit, telling the truth is a revolutionary act"
-Paraphrased from Antonio Gramsci

Introduction

It has been said that the first casualty of war is truth. Here is a truth for starters: In the United States, we are living with the greatest war mongering culture in the history of the world. It has been global domination at any cost. Unfathomable evil has been unleashed and this demon is growing new horns, that is to say murdering new nations of people. This book reveals that these are the same people with the same murderous proclivities that we have witnessed on a global scale since 1492…same perpetrators, same genocide. Since this creature is killing its host, it cannot be associated with parasites as it was interpreted in the 1960s. We will take it a step further. In order to find a cure for the problem, we need to know what the problem is. Allow us to share some brief information from the internet regarding the diagnosis of this behavior.

From cancer.org, we find, "A virus must enter a living cell and "hijack" the cell's machinery in order to reproduce and make more viruses." From cancerquest.org we find, "Through their mutagenic activity or their effects on cell behavior, viruses play a significant role in the development of particular cancers in many different animals, including humans." Independent thinking reveals that the genocidal demons we are dealing with turn out to be viruses rather than parasites. We are concerned with viruses that lead to cancer. This describes not only our relationship to the foreign invading culture, but also its relationship to all other living things. Our survival depends on us being able to recognize a virus in order to neutralize its effect and stop its damage.

This book will deal with potential reasons and motives for genocide so that we can devise solutions that are sustainable. We will share a brief sketch of Dr. Frances Cress-Welsing's thesis relating to this hyper-aggressive virus. From the *Cress Theory of Color Confrontation*, it will be argued that the problem involves genes as well as memes. In other words, we are dealing with more than just a social problem. It is also a genetic problem having to do with the perceived threat of genetic annihilation. The genetic problem of the invader creates other genetic problems. For example, we are at the point of eating genetically modified foods (GMOs) in the U.S. We are being changed biologically against our will. The virus is altering the human family physically, chemically, and biologically. This is not just a cultural problem. From the point of view of people of color, the evidence points to genetic problems leading to other biological disharmony and social chaos.

The 1960s movement dealt primarily with social problems that stem from stealing, killing and destroying that gave rise to dehumanization and inequity. In the United States, the educational system sanitizes and recreates this behavior to be perpetuated domestically and globally. What have we learned about the virus so far? The invading virus hijacks the cells, (which are indigenous people) to reproduce more viruses (which are genocidal invaders). Since the 1960s, the virus has mutated to make us think it is something different. Growing without detection, the virus becomes a cancerous agent of death to most humans in the Global South, but also to all other living things in our eco-system. We know it is the same virus because from 1492 to 2018, we have been continuously invaded by the same perpetrators with the same genocide.

Obviously, we have to stop the onslaught in order to survive. So, what do we do? What is the antidote to the spread of the deadly viral infection? As we learn from the immune system, the first step is to recognize foreign invasion. Then neutralize its effect, expel it from the body, and remember the problem and solution. In practice, the Vietnamese used creativity, unity, and an unrelenting will to defend themselves. Cubans used internal education and international alliances with a country that could help defend them from U.S. aggression. The Kogi in Columbia used isolation to their advantage and kept the invaders out of their language. These are just a few examples. The potential solutions are limitless.

We have to think about what we have that the virus cannot infiltrate and destroy. What do we have that the foreign invading virus does not have? We have soul. It cannot be mistaken or imitated. This is unique to black Americans. Africans are great people, but in reality, they do not have the swagger or soul of black Americans. Our music is called soul music. African music is not. Our food is called soul food. African food is not. Soul is an individual resonance and a group vibration. It is our culture. It is our swagger. Our group vibration comes from our inner diversity as well as our unique struggle. We have to learn and teach the psychological tricks that keep us from controlling our own soulful vibe. That means defense from mentacide, having group pride, understanding what it is going to take for us to stay alive. Currently, the virus controls our learning, teaching, acting, playing, singing, etc. largely because the soulless profit vibration is under its control.

In order to solve the problem, we have to expose the viral infection of continuous deadly aggression so that we can recognize what we are dealing with. What do we have at our disposal that we can use to protect ourselves and our group? The key lies within our soul. Healthy cells have to keep our resonance of soul alive, so the infected cells have a way of knowing when the virus has changed them. If you are black American and do not have any love for black Americans, then you have been infected. If you are a cell who does not work vigorously to keep the body alive, then you have been infected. If you have not realized that we are a nation of people worthy of survival as a group, then you have been infected.

And this book is for you. It has been written to offer wisdom to the healthy and the sick. It has been written for those who are open-minded, but also to nudge those who are closed-minded into a greater place of awareness so that all can survive.

There are endless other dichotomous relationships that this book will cover. For example, this book has been written because we do not seem to understand friend from foe, right from wrong, predator from prey, FBI from comrades, East from West, survival from greed, myth from fact, reality from delusion, logic from emotion, education from indoctrination, freedom from slavery, self-hate from self-love, etc. While not actually dichotomous, we will also explain randomness from determinism in order to help us understand truth from belief. Given that this book contains quite a few poems, do not expect the solutions to always be straight forward. Sometimes the meter, the rhythm in the poems is not straight forward either. We have tried to use layout features to keep the reader on track. In this book, we are going to use language that calls things what they are from the perspective of the black American experience coupled with our best understanding of the laws of nature. This is an example of black American soul. Soul is revolutionary. Soul is connected to Mother Earth. Soul is magical. Our unique and internally diversified soul makes unity, creativity, and the will to survive as a group possible. This is our wellspring for reversing genocide.

The title of this book is broadly generic because many of the solutions to genocide are the same whether the problem is in the Americas, Africa, the Middle East, or elsewhere. Common problems among victims of genocidal aggression include stolen land and resources, murder of insurgents, propaganda, infiltration, creation of poverty, creation of chaos, financial indebtedness, psychological and emotional manipulation, and hiding the culprit to make it seem as if the victims are doing it to themselves. Consequently, the choices of perpetual servitude or death create hopelessness that leads to other mental and physiological problems such as self-hate and/or drug addiction. Since this book is written more specifically for black Americans, we also cover slavery more so than colonization because slavery includes the loss of cultural memory and hybridization which includes a loss of identity. We will demonstrate in the following pages that these debilitating, inhumane problems are primarily the result of violence and deception. At the core of solutions is self-education (individual and collective self) as well as international alliances.

We assume that the reader is already familiar with the basics of the problem and we build on this knowledge rather than just introducing it. In the interest of brevity, we leave out details of topics covered in our first book, *Elusive Quest for Freedom*. This more recent book is probably not a good first read for a person who has not already been exposed to the deception of nearly all mainstream information we receive in U.S. society. Almost everything we learn is narrated and interpreted to be opposite the truth. For those who have not already recognized this, we recommend reading *Elusive Quest for Freedom* before reading *Reversing Genocide*. This is not a feel-good book, but it does have some elements that make it fun. It is the ultimate self-help book which stretches help for the individual self all the way to help for the group-self, then to the end goal of sovereign thinking and sovereign control. In the last volume, we started with invasion. This time we will just introduce invasion so that we can start the main body of material with more liberating interpretations of freedom.

Understanding the order of invasion helps us to come to grips with the current world order within which we struggle for the flowering of our humanity. In terms of the European invasion of the Global South, which defines the aggressor-victim order, we should consider the process by which this came about. First, they come in and pretend to be friends. Deception typically precedes violence. But, ultimately the aggressors, here defined as Europeans and Jews, come to murder people in order to steal the land and resources. There was no serious consideration toward finding a way to live sustainably in their homeland. Once they destroyed their land with demented ecological views and destructive environmental practices, the solution has been to steal land from other people, not to change their ways and improve their practices.

After stealing the land and resources, the second order of aggression is to steal the political economy. There is no politics without an economy and there is no economy without politics. Disaggregated, these two topics make no sense. That is precisely why we are taught these subjects separate from each other. Compartmentalized instruction keeps us from making important connections leaving us unable to figure out what is really going on. The political portion of this topic includes not only governance, but also defense. The aggressor moves in to take away the victim's ability to defend its group. The U.S. and Israel do not want anyone in the Global South to have nuclear weapons so that people of color are not able to defend themselves against white aggression. Clearly, this has disastrous results as we have seen in Libya. The economic component of this topic includes labor and trade. Slave labor and colonialism are obvious, but trade wars and control by banks are less obvious.

Once a group's landed resources and political economies are stolen, the third order of aggression is to steal the education of the children. As previously noted, the behavior of the invading virus is to teach the healthy cells to act like them. That is to say to teach children the benefits and greatness of the invader's ways to cause them to desire to be like the aggressor. Most victims of invasion will not be able to successfully emulate the invader. Most will remain poor and inferior versions of the virus. But even a successful virus is still a virus. The result is still self-destruction. Indigenous people will not be allowed to be themselves except to the extent that it entertains, enriches, or defends the invader. For example, black Americans are celebrated when they are known as Buffalo Soldiers or Tuskegee Airmen. Warmongers love you if you go to war for them. When the education is taken over, the children are taught to produce the same kind of results as the invader. Healthy, sustainable practices are lost to deadly, inhumane ways of thinking and living.

The fourth order of aggression is to cause indigenous people to give up their culture of food and medicine production. The children are taught to grow food for profit, not for nourishment. Combining economics, education, and food production, we see how Haiti went from being a net food exporter to a net food importer long before the recent earthquake. Although Haiti freed the land back in 1790, we see the other three orders of aggression still in play. The takeover of the political economy has been there at least since Papa Doc, Baby Doc, and the removal of Aristide. This ensures that miseducation and under-education will be rampant. Consequently, the banks come in to the finish the kill with bending the food markets toward the profiteers and away from the benefit of the people.

One of the lessons to be learned here is that the absence of chattel slavery is not freedom. Haiti is obviously not free. In the U.S., slavery was officially abolished in 1865 but that does not mean that slaves became free. The end of slavery is not the beginning of freedom. It is only a step in the direction of freedom. It is rather like starting a marathon of 26 miles, but we have only run one mile. We are a long way from completing the race. We would not call the removal of shackles freedom just like we would not call one mile a marathon. Freedom is still a long way from being achieved for people of color in the United States. That is the purpose of this book. We intend to lay the foundation for a path that leads to group freedom. It should be clear that individual freedom does not exist outside of group freedom. We learn that group survival is impossible, which leaves us to only pursue individual survival. To put it very succinctly, individualism, as taught in this society, is a deceptive trick to perpetuate servitude.

We will include several poems that drive this point home. You will find some redundancy in the poems. They have been purposely written to cover the same topic from different angles. Some people may not get it from one angle but may get it from another. So, there is an attempt to reach a broad audience of people who are willing to recognize the reality of conditions that we live in. Once we recognize the reality of who we are, where we are, and what is going on, we can begin to actually start to solve the problem of European and Jewish domination. Some of the language in this book is harsh and some would consider it extreme. The reason is that we have to compensate for the most cancerous agent of death in human history. We are not going to be able to slip and slide out of this problem of genocide. It is an extreme problem and it will take extreme language and actions to overcome this Earth-destroying virus.

This book is untraditional in that it contains several styles of writing and graphics as well. There are poems, short stories, speeches, essays, diagrams, tables, outlines, and prose. We attempt to weave this together in a fluid way that is readable and informative. We hope that you find it engaging and useful. Through the many different genres, there is a consistent thesis. While the main focus is about the freedom and survival of one group in particular, this struggle has the power to free the world of European and Jewish global domination. Global domination is an Earth destroying desire regardless of the people who attempt it.

We tend to leave out details on topics that are covered in other books; but we offer references for further study. The last chapters of the book (in volume two) are shorter because much of the material for these sections is covered as we move through the early chapters. We hope that intuitively, logically, or visually you will be able to come beyond your preconceived notions about the conditions of oppressed people. Survival and sustainability require us to be open to more harmonious ways of looking at the world. This book is intended to help us to see beyond the Euro-Jewish limitations that we have been confined to. Along these lines, we will share something to keep in mind as you read through this book. To the best of our knowledge, the following quote originated with Tupac Amaru Shakur:

"…Real Eyes
 …Realize
 …Real Lies."

"You never change things by fighting the existing reality. To change something, build a new model that makes the existing model obsolete."

-Buckminster Fuller

Chapter 1   Interpretations of Freedom

Wrong Side of History

We need not be on the wrong side of history
  When the Chinese tiger pounces
    She might not formally announce it
And we are already at the bottom where we can hardly breathe
  This is not a joke
When the anti-nature system comes crashing down
  The buffer group at the bottom gets destroyed the most
    We don't want to be on the wrong side of history
Crony capitalism is married to a plutocracy
  As the mask comes off our pseudo-democracy
Now, socialism is on the rise and communalism is coming back
  We have to step up to the plate
    And not act like it is our first time up to bat
      Putting money in black banks is just the beginning of that
From here, we start with Claud Anderson's Powernomics
  And then move on
    To the more communal oriented Participatory Economics
We have to start building some trust
  And recognizing what works for us
    We don't want to be on the wrong side of history
We find the cloak of Middle Eastern religions
  To be torn and tattered
Since oppressed people are beginning to see again
  What the real things in life are that matter
Don't be on the wrong side of reality, reason, and revolution
  We have the wealth, knowledge, and labor
    To build our own institutions

The first thing we have to do is teach group survival over greed
  So that we can create for ourselves
    The opportunities we really need
It is imperative that we have land on which to survive
  When the music stops, we don't want to be the only ones
    With no land from which to rise
      But we first have to be connected to the land on the inside
We have to know beyond a doubt where we belong
  We don't want our children's side of history to be wrong
We could be learning to pull out our inner greatness
  Instead of learning the status quo
Mainstream teachings confine the refinement of our minds
  By narrowing the view of what we know
We don't want to be on the blind side of history
  We cannot survive
    Thinking that life is just one of God's mysteries
Life has to be lived for real
  If we respect and love each other right here, right now
    How divine will that feel?
Rather than working for unity
  Maybe we should work against destabilization
We have to recognize the opposition to organizing
  And expose bribery temptations
    Or any other way we can reduce complications
The hot topic now is violent repression
  And if I may make a suggestion
Freeing ourselves from European and Jewish domination
  Is not out of the question
We have to change the rules of engagement
  To keep our bodies from growing cold on the pavement
Just as the invader prepares and trains to murder the youth
  We have to prepare and train to protect our group
Like the Vietnamese, we have to internalize unity, creativity
  And an unrelenting will to defend our people
    Only then will we ever be respected as equals
      We don't want to be on the wrong side of history
Police murders could lead us to unity
  Causing us to look back inward to the community

We have to encourage our people to rise
  To another level in awareness of self
    Ice cold barriers to black unity will begin to melt
We are going to have to change the rules and develop new tools
  As Victims Of Oppression Do Unite
We don't want to be on the wrong side
  Of a ruinous historical plight
So, how are we going to win?
  Victims Of Oppression Do Unite. Recognize the acronym
This will help us through
  The first letter of each word spells: VOODU

Here we are more than sixty years past the origin of the Civil Right Movement and we are still allowing our resistance to domination to be controlled by the very same people who are dominating us. This is ludicrous. We are not fighting for survival. We are fighting to fit in. This describes the difference between revolution and reform which is also the difference between freedom and Civil Rights. Our problem of perpetual slavery cannot be reformed away. Following the logic of the quote that we began with, we will have to focus more on making our own rules than on changing the foreign invader's rules. Just like our immune system, the first step in solving the problem of invasion is being able to recognize what is foreign. A more liberating perspective in the U.S. exposes that Europeans are not Americans, for example. They are foreign invaders of America. We have to remember like T-cells who are foreign in order to heal ourselves. From the logic in our introduction, we conclude that Europeans and Jews are the virus that brought genocide and destruction to America and continues to weaken our immune response. Now, the virus is infecting the Middle East with the same deplorable and reprehensible behavior. Contrary to our thinking about the post-Civil Rights era, the foreign invading murderers have not changed their ways at home or abroad.

In hindsight, we can tell by the outcome where the domination comes from. We can see which policies are being pursued and which are being advanced, domestically and internationally. We are going to use language and perspectives that deal with the moral philosophy of policies and actions that primarily come from the United States and Israel. Practical moral philosophy is necessarily political and strategic. Moral philosophy is not just religious as we tend to associate morality with religion. For example, Dr. King taught that we had a moral duty to disobey unjust laws. This is political and strategic. We realize at this point that we have to combine this approach with the statement popularized by Malcolm X, "by any means necessary." Updating this phrase, we realize that all means are necessary.

In this book, we will bring several things forward from the movement of the 1960s as well as from our previous work entitled, *Elusive Quest for Freedom*. One of the ideas we brought forward was the rhetoric about parasites. We have come to know that our adversary is better described as a virus. This is of paramount importance because if we leave any openings for the virus to enter, it will infiltrate, infect, grow, and destroy. We can be absolutely sure about this, not only because of what it has done, but also because of what it continues to do without restraint or remorse. For this reason, we have to learn to defend ourselves by all means necessary. The language in this book is carefully chosen to reflect the liberation of black Americans which is pivotal to the liberation of the world.

Given that we are terrestrial animals, we must secure territory in order to win the fight for survival. Since we are social animals, this is a group effort. When a famous entertainer took all her clothes off in Dallas, she spoke about getting away from group thinking. While it is important to be able to think independently, those independent thoughts should still benefit the individual and the group as well as the environment. The outcome of our actions shows us whether behavior is group-oriented or from a mindset of individual greed. Our actions always affect the group whether we intend to or not. We should be consciously aware of the fact that the group must survive in order for the individual to truly survive. A mindset of balanced effort has to be in place for liberation.

We certainly want to avoid the slippery slope of individualism which is one of the tactics used successfully against us. As long as we do not see ourselves as a group, as long as we do not have any collective consciousness, the masses of our black American group will continue to be oppressed. Large masses of people are oppressed by keeping them away from group power. Without group defense, open season on black people will continue. Wealthy black people have a false sense of security because history has shown that this subgroup is not safe either. We have to include both individual and group participation to teach and develop a meaningful view of the end game so that our organizations for activism are headed in a particular, sustained direction that includes defense. The end goal has to be clear and has to include a comprehensive plan of defense. In other words, freedom has to be well defined and understood by all victims of oppression. We will cover this thoroughly in the pages that follow.

In the last few decades, we have celebrated the presumed progress we have made socially and economically without a balanced, critical view of our lack of progress toward freedom. Clearly, we are still dominated by the same people who controlled us at the beginning of the Civil Rights Movement. Obviously, we have still not become free; nor are we actually on a path toward freedom. Some will argue that our social and economic progress demonstrates that we have a greater degree of freedom than we had under Jim Crow laws prior to the 1960s. As an analogy, Malcolm X taught us that pulling a knife out of my back is not freedom. Progress toward freedom does not begin until the wound begins to heal.

Although we have a larger middle class and more black millionaires, this is not evidence that the wound has begun to heal. Given the thesis of *The New Jim Crow by Michelle Alexander*, the knife is still in our backs although it has been pulled out to some degree. In some ways we have attained a greater degree of comfort; but the wound has not begun to heal and, therefore, we are not secure in our ability to survive. A greater degree of comfort is not automatically a greater degree of freedom. We cannot heal ourselves without a sovereign food supply, sovereign justice system, sovereign schools, a sovereign medical infrastructure, etc. As long as we allow mass murder, mass incarceration, and mass miseducation to continue unabated, the wound has not begun to heal. This leads us into the next poem.

Police murder

Murder, mass incarceration, and miseducation
   Madmen of malevolent machinations
Making mayhem of mankind
   Machiavellian mischief molding minds
Resulting in death and destruction with impunity
   Stopping all independent progress in the community
We have to change the laws
   For a righteous cause
In order to change the way they treat our kind
   We have to start with a "never again" strategy in mind
The badges and incidents of slavery keep us backing up
   Stuck in a seemingly powerless rut
The NAACP has worked on this problem for decades
   And cannot seem to get it solved
They are either guided by oppressive perpetrators or
   Up against an impenetrable wall
As local police remain above reproach
   Our leaders are boxed into a civil rights approach

While we are continually invaded by the devil's cohorts
   Who brutalize and kill us for sport
And we are led to believe that we can win
   By simply taking them to court
It's like asking the chicken hawk to guard the hen house
   There is no wonder why the masses still have doubt
About the outcome of this asymmetrical game
   In spite of an occasional guilty verdict
     The aggression on the street remains the same
A police conviction here and there doesn't bring systemic change
   Without remorse or change of course
     Poor people of color are murdered without shame
We got a conviction in Florida
   Where the music was allegedly too loud
     This is one out of hundreds, so how can we feel proud?
We are still being murdered on almost a daily basis
   While our struggle is confined
     To the winning of a few court cases
That really makes a mockery of our attempt to fight
  At the end of the tunnel, we still can't see the light
     Something ain't right
We may very well have a black police chief
   But that doesn't necessarily give us any relief
Even supporting and voting for a black mayor
   Won't ameliorate the conditions of the low end tax payer
That's why Mumia Abu Jamal said
   Even when we win elections...we lose
     Murderous police are found innocent through subterfuge
We are stuck in a game in which we only have pawns to move
  Marching and begging and singing the blues
   We persistently and frequently continue to be abused
We have to think harder about proposed solutions
   That never actually brings us remedy or restitution

European aggression has been extremely hard to stop
   Our attempts at liberation are maliciously blocked
Which begs the question, what good is voting
   If we cannot vote them out?
What kind of freedom are we winning
   If we are still left impotent and without clout?
We don't see ourselves as worthy of a "never again" plan
   We only see ourselves begging for justice
     As if we are making meaningful demands
This is where miseducation comes in
   Placating educated blacks with insignificant battles they can win
Never actually changing the structure of control
   Expecting benevolence or justice from creatures with no soul
Leaving us tricked by some kind of multicultural, rainbow blend
   Still unable to defend ourselves
     In a way that we can say "never again"
We have been terrorized by Europeans for hundreds of years
   By incessant, merciless violence to maintain a climate of fear
Mass murder, mass incarceration, and miseducation
   Parts of a demonic culture to maintain European domination
We are confused and afraid to consider
   What a "never again" outcome looks like
In order to make it truly right...in order to truly make it right
   Black Americans should "never again" be policed by whites

Since we are still suffering from the same violent repression that has been a persistent part of our existence with Europeans, the knife analogy and this first poem expose our need for a collective view of what progress is. Let us weave together a working understanding of progress, freedom, and degrees of freedom. We will certainly have to meet incremental goals as we work toward freedom; but we need not confuse ourselves about degrees. In this work, we will define freedom simply as self-control, individually and collectively. Impotent black political figure heads in the same system of exploitation does not qualify as self-control. Corporations essentially control their decisions, miseducation controls their ambitions, and ego controls a corruptible quest for power. Black people, who have been trained to think and act like oppressors, make decisions for other black people that do not liberate victims of invasion and subjugation. Black faces in high places do not bring equality to the races. Our leadership has to be controlled by black culture and black values, not just by black faces.

Individual self-control requires knowledge of self and self-discipline. Collective self-control requires knowledge of the group-self and group discipline. The black American group we refer to is primarily a southern Atlantic ecological group of people indigenous to the Western Hemisphere. Collective self-control involves the cultural foundation of peoples from the southern Atlantic. Specifically, this means the common culture from eastern America, the Caribbean, and western Africa. This is the same culture that the Moors were a part of when they brought Columbus to the Americas. Collective self-control means cultural self-discipline and tenacity. With an understanding that we must remain adaptable, we must adhere to and never lose sight of our core principles as a people. This adhesiveness provides cohesiveness while helping to mitigate and minimize internecine strife and protect us from externally imposed controls. Freedom from internal and external sabotage is an important ingredient of liberation, particularly since the U.S. is very well adept with infiltrating and destroying.

It goes without saying that any version of freedom has to be defended. This defense has to be comprehensive enough to include a "never again" strategy. We have to be able to defend ourselves before we can seriously entertain ideas of progress. We can define progress for this discussion as the incremental accomplishments toward the end goal of self-control and defense of that control. We have to deal with sovereignty in order to have meaningful discussions about justice. Neely Fuller Jr.'s thesis is about producing justice and we will refer to his work several times. We agree with his dismantling the illusion of white supremacy as a part of producing justice. The topic of justice has not been treated effectively because we cannot realistically produce justice until we have secured control of our own minds, our own cultural values, and our own legal system. In order to produce justice, we require the raw materials of production which begins with understanding what justice is. The first input in the production of justice is to define what justice is. That means we have to interpret what justice is and enforce it for ourselves. Being at the mercy of an oppressor's sense of justice is a prescription for failure. Since oppression is unjust, expecting justice from a system of oppression is delusional. In light of historical relationships over the last several hundred years, it becomes apparent that our freedom and defense of that freedom requires sovereignty. Sovereignty enables the wherewithal to produce justice.

To get to the end of 1865, we required a military as allies to move toward ending our dehumanization in order to make some progress toward the goal of freedom. In order to become a healthy people, we have to be able to become free from continuous European aggression. Progress is only made when young black people are taught how to become free of European and Jewish violence and deception. Presently, we remain under a brutal system of domination. Education is our second input in the production of justice. By this we mean a relevant, southern Atlantic education. We are an internally diverse people trying to survive in America. Our education has to be different from the foreign invader trying to dominate America…and the world. If we are intellectually locked into a domination paradigm, then we will not be able to produce justice because we have not received an education that has prepared us to do so. As Carter G. Woodson wrote, "When you can control a man's thinking, you don't have to worry about his actions."

We are making the case that we require an infrastructure for the production of justice. Mental scaffolding is required. Part of the scaffolding is offered in this writing. First, we have to define justice. Second, we have to teach justice. Third, we cannot produce justice without a legal system to produce it in (fertile ground). We cannot produce justice out of the unjust legal system of the foreign invader which is a virus what will continue to mutate anytime we gain advantages. Therefore, we cannot reform its problems away. We have to develop a system that works for us where we are the majority. Politically speaking, we have to make rules that liberate us and interpret them according to our view of justice. We obviously have irreconcilable differences with the dominant culture in this regard. In other words, this third input into the production of justice is a social infrastructure that enables liberating and sustainable group work. As quoted in the beginning, we have to build a new model. If we continue to be educated for exploitation, that is what we will continue to do even if we become politically free. Injustice will persist.

Another thing that black Americans seem to be delusional about is what the requirements are for our survival into the future. Being temporarily treated fairly does not necessarily improve our ability to survive. Neither does being temporarily granted equality. These outcomes do not change the power dynamic between the oppressor and the oppressed. We seem to think that if they treat us better, then we are no longer oppressed. Let us offer something that may sharpen our perspective on where equality and entrepreneurship fit into a liberation strategy with an end game of self-control (full sovereignty). Equality is not related to freedom, particularly when that equality is granted or denied by the oppressor.

Only two sovereign groups, who can defend themselves, can come to the negotiating table as equals. Therefore, equality requires sovereignty. Of course, freedom also includes economic independence. Entrepreneurship in a capitalist system is not economic freedom. We must have economic control over our own lives and resources; but without the same inequitable capitalist exploitation. Instead of another group taking advantage of us, we do it to ourselves as we emulate the oppressor in business relations. Greed rather than survival has been the driving force. This drives us apart and drives the masses of our people into deeper poverty and external control. Black-owned economic production leads toward self-sufficiency. This is not the same as the Capitalist business model of greed, which is known to sell us out and ultimately destroy any plans of freedom and equality. Inequality is inherent in the Capitalist model.

As part of this discussion, we have noted that comfort is not freedom. This is a major psychological obstacle for wealthy blacks. Neely Fuller Jr. says comfort is not justice and I think we capture the same idea as we write about freedom. The fact that we have a larger black middle class and more millionaires does not mean we have made progress toward freedom. The same murderous thieves remain in control of our millionaires and middle class. Our material advancement only pushes them higher which means our relative position remains the same. Also, because of the Capitalist model, we also have a larger group in poverty. We have fewer black businesses, fewer black banks, and less unity with racial pride. In addition, the wealth can be taken away at any time.

Much of our hard-earned gains from the 1960s and 1970s evaporated with the crack epidemic of the 1980s as new Jim Crow tactics were maliciously implemented. Then, of course, we were hit harder by the financial crisis of 2008 than other groups as we were fleeced by predatory lenders into believing we could afford larger homes with subpar credit. Many black neighborhoods never recovered. This wealth was taken away and redistributed to hedge funds for the wealthy. It was a transfer of wealth from middle class communities to very wealthy people.

It should be clear at this point that comfort is not freedom. Pets can be made comfortable. That does not make them free. The notable mental and emotional condition is that pets do not want to become free largely because of their comfort. Their ability to survive is diminished. Their fight for survival is nullified. This pet analogy describes black people in the U.S. who have good jobs, well-paying self-employment, or own successful businesses. Black American progress can only be measured, in aggregate, by changes in autonomy and defense, not by a larger class of consumers that give their new-found wealth right back to the oppressor, so they can be comfortable. This has long since been called financing our own oppression. Black wealth has not translated into black freedom because we have not developed the mental and spiritual prerequisites to liberation. In order for black wealth to be useful, it has to lead toward black sovereignty. Recall the demise of black Wall Street in Tulsa, Oklahoma. Toward developing a working definition of freedom, we have tried to demonstrate that justice requires sovereignty, that equality is not freedom, entrepreneurship is not freedom, and comfort is not freedom.

Freedom, sovereignty, and self-control are on a different path than Civil Rights and equality. We are trying to move from the scripted equality track to the freedom of the survival track. Recognition of the group self which includes group love and group discipline is a prominent key to our survival. Self-hate, greed, and neutrality maintain the status quo which ensures that we remain a perpetually subordinated group. Perpetual slavery is one way to view our current condition. We intend to challenge your thinking about how we get from this state of servitude to a state of self-rule. This book primarily deals with the antagonistic and asymmetrical relationship between European invaders and the perpetually subordinated group of internally diverse people called black. Since we are familiar with referencing people by color, keep in mind that many of the aggression issues from pale people not only affect black people, but also negatively affect the humanity of red and brown people as well.

With that being said, however, we also know that the interests of historically Spanish (Hispanic) people, who are the complexion of southern Europeans, will be advanced over and above the indigenous and imported people of color. All colored people are not treated the same resulting from a strategic hierarchy. Noticeably, the brown skinned people from India do not suffer the same oppression in the U.S. of indigenous groups, especially those mixed with African. This is because the problem of perpetual violent aggression does not actually stem from us being of a different hue. The problem stems from having something that European and Jewish invaders want to steal.

The stealing typically involves land (resources) and/or labor, but also includes intellectual capital as well. Killing and destruction are an integral part of the mission to create a situation in which they will never have to give back what they stole from people of color in the Global South. With respect to color, we will take a different path for the use of the word race. We will lean on insight from Claud Anderson. The so-called racial tragedy is really about the race for resources which involves the torture, terror, and destruction of indigenous and ecological groups. It is within this context that we can truly understand the past and begin to plan for a more sustainable and harmonious future. Tyranny is not sustainable, and this describes the conditions that we are living with currently in 2018.

The information put forth here is unapologetically an indictment of Euro-Jewish aggression which is a problem that remains unresolved. While the overwhelming majority of Europeans in the U.S. are complicit beneficiaries of violent aggression, we are not implicating all Europeans in absolute terms. We might roughly estimate that there is about 1% of this group actively working against the aggression of their own ecological group. We may liberally assume there are another 4% who have, through close associations with blacks or through extensive research, overcome white supremacy. This category of people is well meaning and altruistic and also believes in equality. They do not, however, believe in black independence. They may accept the idea of reparations as long as it does not upset the status quo. They will not, however, entertain the moral and economic rebalancing of restitution. This is a current problem to solve in South Africa.

Then there are a very large number of those who are apathetic about or indifferent to the consequences of European aggression. They go along to get along. They are complicit and comfortable. Even so-called poor whites are comfortable with the white supremacist idea that at least they are above black people. This group is unknowingly impressionable. They believe what they learned in school is at least close to the truth. They believe what they see on the news is at least close to unbiased and accurate reporting. This group thinks that they are neutral and believes in democracy, even though they are comfortable with joining the military to further undemocratic aggression.

Beyond this, there is a large group of so-called whites who actually hate black people. We estimate 9%. This is how we end up with the constant problem of murdered black people, mostly with impunity. It is not only a systemic, state sanctioned problem of violent repression, but it also includes random acts of violence as in the case of George Zimmerman or Dylan Roof or Michael Dunn. Apparently, it is from this group that many police officers are chosen. It is empirically true that white supremacist groups have grown tremendously since Barak Obama became President. Finally, there is the top 1% of European and Jewish invaders whom we will not accuse of hating black people because they are mostly heartless demons who seem to function without emotion. They do not care about hate or love. They are singularly concerned with attaining the power of global domination. Allow us to share a table that illustrates this view from a visual perspective.

1%	4%	85%	9%	1%
Active	Passive	Passive	Active	Active
Constructive	Go with the flow	Go with the flow	Destructive	Destructive
Freedom Fighters	Aware but defeatist	Neutral	Oligarchy	Plutocracy
Equality, Justice	Complicit	Apathetic, Ambivalent	Corporate heads	Social engineers
Indigenous Focus		Complicit	Politicians	
		Critical mass		
		Herding instinct		

In order to clear the air of any energy from this writing related to hate or bigotry, we need to share some brief thoughts on group behavior and critical mass. When we expose the naked aggression of mostly western Europeans and Jews, we are not implying that it is all people in the ecological or religious group. We are suggesting that it is enough of them to maintain the status quo. It is enough of them to keep black people as a perpetual underclass. It is enough to allow the extra judicial killing of black people as a normal functioning part of this society's law enforcement activities. While it may not be all so-called white people, there is a critical mass of invaders who are not only complicit with maintaining the problem, but many are actually active in supporting it. BrainyQuote.com has the following from Will Durant, "It may be true that you can't fool all the people all the time, but you can fool enough of them to rule a large country. "The same critical mass allows genocide in the Middle East. Many are comfortable with the ideology of supporting our troops, which is the same hyper-aggressive violence that gave rise to this demonic political entity in the first place. Same virus. Same harbingers of death.

    The system, which is only briefly sketched in the table above, tips in favor of those at the top because they get critical mass by using extremely aggressive energy and psychological manipulation to lead the larger population in their direction. Humans are herders, so most of us follow. When we disagree, we are still trapped in the system. We have been confined to making incremental changes to the current system in hopes of reaching critical mass someday. We tend to lean towards the larger, invading, European population to get critical mass. Although they are a majority in the U.S., they are a minority in the world. In spite of being a small group, they use the energy of violence and deception to sway the masses of people. Military, monetary, and miseducation (particularly with respect to religion) are the primary tools of dominating people's energy into mass following. The direction of our energy is programmed by the architects and purveyors of the system. The culture is pitched to us as if it is heavenly, celebrity, manifest destiny, written in the stars.

Star Spangled

The United States of genocide
  Causing the gates of hell to open wide
Indigenous people from all over the world trapped inside
  Overworked and undernourished, barely alive
Robbed of the raw materials we need to survive
  Including the teachings of our forebears that enabled us to thrive
Instead, we are given white supremacy to imbibe
  From the world's most violent tribe

Then we are actually expected to join the military
  Or, at least, go along for the ride
As we are mentally and physically destroyed
  Trying to hold it all inside
Our efforts at unity and autonomy have been destroyed
  Every time we have tried
So, we are unable to provide well for our families
  Unless we shuck and jive
Accepting a capitalist-slavery guide
  We end up selling our own people out as we take the bribes
And even though we know in our hearts that this is not wise
  We justify it by blaming the victims or other delusions and lies
We cannot even trust our families in which to confide
  Because our communities have been flooded
    With so many agents and spies
Some have tried to escape to Africa, but there is nowhere to hide
  We have tried to hold our heads high
    But we end up swallowing our pride
Forced into yet another concession or compromise
  So that we will be left with nothing from which to rise
Given the military and PsyOps are gargantuan in size
  Our condition comes as no surprise
Yet, against what appears to be insurmountable odds,
  We have to realize
That we can still overcome if we keep our eyes
  On a fully independent prize

We are aware that there are some beautiful Europeans in this country who do understand fairness and equality. But, we also know that there are not enough of them to turn this boat around. There remains a critical mass of European invaders armed to the teeth who, very undemocratically, never intend to relinquish power to any other people whether they become the majority or not.

There is the fear that others will take over the country. For example, we mentioned there was a significant spike in the growth of white supremacist groups when Barak Obama became President. We can be assured that black people in the U.S. have no intention of ever taking over this country. We do not want to rule white people. We only want to take over our own lives. Our survival depends on it. This also reveals how we can be so clear on the devilish mentality that seeks to destroy us when we attempt to control our own lives. It should be understood that Europeans in the U.S. do not fight against black people taking over. They fight against black people having some say in our own lives. They fight to maintain black slavery.

This analysis reveals that it is not possible for us to connect with the critical mass of Europeans in the U.S. as a strategy toward liberation. In other words, the 99% fight is not our fight because the 99% still want us enslaved. Or, at least, a critical mass of this group is complicit with our perpetual servitude. While the majority of Europeans in the U.S. may want to be free of the control of the 1%, that does not imply that they want black people to be free of white rule. Recently, there has been a great deal of conversation centered on poor whites and poor blacks fighting together against the wealthiest class. This may very well be a necessary struggle, but we cannot lose sight of the fact that this does not free blacks from whites. A favorable outcome only frees blacks from the wealthiest whites.

We listened to a short message from T.D. Jakes who defined "comrades" as people who are against what you are against. But they are not for what you are for. This captures the spirit of the poor people's campaign in which both poor whites and poor blacks are against the hoarding of wealth by the 1%, but poor whites are not for the sovereignty of blacks. Given its resurgence, it is important that we understand the limitations of the poor people's campaign. We will share a poem that explains the fight of the 99% is really not the fight of black people in this country.

13%
Mumia Abu Jamal said that we are so far behind
  We don't even know where the starting line is
    We may not be in Oz, but we have been tricked by the Wiz
So, let's talk about where this thing starts
  Like watching the stars navigate the night sky
    And drawing cave art
Telling stories about our beginning and future
  Later learning to write scriptures and sutras
So that we could pass down knowledge of our past
  To ensure that our culture and communities last
Unfortunately, all of this can be interrupted by invasion
  And change the balance of the equation
    Giving rise to retarded relations
Distorting what we know
  Locking us into a self-destructive flow
Naturally, we have to look beyond foreign control
  To find out what our ancestors were told
As they learned from the sky and the Earth
  How to value their self-worth
Not from genocidal maniacs claiming to be superior
  With unfathomable violence piercing to our mental interior
Boxing in our thoughts so that truth cannot be found
  As we are on the precipice of global catastrophe
    It is well past time to turn things around
Most of us know that we are killing ourselves
  But we have not learned how to make heaven out of hell
One thing we need to know about is the spirit of the land
  So, we have to get our heads out of the Middle Eastern sand

That includes Christianity, Islam, and the Egyptian system too
   There are pyramids in the U.S.
     That can help us understand what to do
Know this…
Integrating with those who murder and mistreat us
   Mainly Anglo Saxons
     Is a sickness, not a solution nor an intelligent course of action
God blessed the child who has his own
   Is a cliché from back in the days
It starts with our own spirituality
   And then extends to our political-economic ways
All that garbage that comes from mainstream is Satan in disguise
   Full of lies, crippling compromise, and contributes to our demise
If black lives really matter, why are we still begging for rights?
   Liberation means independence
     Which is the only solution to this plight
If young people are going to be on the front lines
   Make sure the outcome is worth the fight
Just because you have heard of nationalism before
   Doesn't make these words rhetorical or trite
Black Christian Nationalism, Republic of New Africa,
   And the Nation of Islam
     All have foreign roots and, therefore, do not solidify our bond
We are an indigenous and unique people with biodiversity inside
   Upon this identity, we can unify and find a way to survive
While we are part of the 99%, we are also the Black 13%
   Who are killed every 28 hours by the European 72%
     So stop straddling the fence
Sure we have some common struggles
   But we have some uncommon issues as well
Like the New Jim Crow which encourages too many of us to fail
   So we can be locked away in jail cells
Everything won't be okay just because we decide to buy black

As the Tulsa race riots demonstrated
   We have to be ready for the attack
It's not just the 1%...
Because the 72% of invading Europeans
  Are the most violent people in human history
We have to account for this
  If we want to achieve a sustainable victory
You are not going to love them into peace
  They will kill you like they did Dr. King
    It should be obvious that we need to wake up from the dream
And realize we have been duped into believing
  In false and antiquated myths
    Keeping us from actualizing the full potential of our gifts
We are embracing the invader's religion
  And feeling spiritually relieved
    Without acknowledging the terrorist roots of what we believe
We are losing this psycho-spiritual battle
  Without realizing we are being deceived
If we cannot figure out when we are being deceived
  Then how can we overcome?
    How can we repair the damage that has been done?
How can the battle for freedom be won?
  And how can we truly protect our young?
If deception is used to repress us, then truth can make us free
  Instead of begging for rights, independence should be our plea
It starts with recognizing the lies within religion
  Which are not God given
Realities have been falsified
  In order to control our lives
For example, we know the Earth is our Mother
  But not that the Sun is our Father
    We think we already have the truth, so we don't bother
We don't take the time to seek and find

The truths that our ancestors considered Divine
Internalized self-hate is so strong
  That we really don't understand right from wrong
    And that's how we end up with misogyny in our songs
Locking up the men and degrading the women
  We may as well be the poor, bombed out victims of Yemen
All money is not good pay
  And joining the U.S. aggression is not the way
Death is more dignified
  At least our dignity won't be compromised
Fighting wars for the top 1%
  And then when all your money is spent
You have to enlist all over again
  Still without seeing your sell-out sins
Even fighting with the 99%
  They will use us, confuse us and then turn their backs
Which will still leave us in the same situation
  Miseducated, impotent, and isolated blacks
The 13% is our fight
  And only independence will make it right
Then we do not have to worry about those who hate and trick us
  Those who look down on us with white supremacist disgust
The 99% fight will still leave us with false hopes of integration
  Unable to contribute to our survival by building a black nation
We can come together to stop the tyranny
  But I want to make sure you are hearin' me
It needs to be emphatically clear that at the end of the day
  We are going our own way

    One thing to take away from this poem is that the poor people's campaign may be a united front, but at the end of the struggle black people still require a sovereign nation in order to survive. We can fight with poor European invaders, but our end goal is still to be free of all classes of European and Jewish domination. We seek to be free from the yoke of poor whites as well. It is not just the 1% that came here to steal. All white people came here to steal, that is to say to partake in the spoils of war and genocide. It should be mentioned that historically the struggle of poor whites has been defused by putting them in charge of black people. It is also poor whites who stand ready to murder us for the 1% such as Dylan Roof in South Carolina. We do not mince words in this book because a sanitized approach does not generate the energy necessary to ignite black people to a struggle for survival. This writing uses language to help us stay focused. It attempts to solve problems with the use of liberation language with respect to the black American struggle for freedom. The following poem uses an acronym to explain Black American Liberation Language.

Freedom's BALL

Freedom's BALL
  Comes from hearing the spirits call
Inspiring with Black American Liberation Language
  Our future looks bleak, but we know we can change it
Rearrange it with limitless creativity from the inside
  On a mission with repetition so we can keep our eyes on the prize
Once we truly realize that we are oppressed as a group
  We will be willing to make the sacrifices necessary
    To teach our youth
Something other than individual success
  While they hold their pompous heads high
    Like slaves that are blessed
But, nonetheless still slaves because the group is still down
  At least until we finally decide to really turn things around
How is the battle against a divide and conquer strategy won?
  Educate our people to unify, and then we can overcome

We have to define freedom with clarity
  In order to overcome the disparity
We have to think in terms of an unwavering commitment to the end
  Because sticking together is the only way we can win
What good is a poem if it doesn't encourage us to get unified?
  What good is group education
    If our group problems can't be rectified?
What good is music if we don't sing any freedom songs?
  As the rhythms of self-destruction
    Keep us from even recognizing right from wrong
Freedom is not individual success; it is self-control
  From this definition, we can develop strategic goals
Of course, I am talking about the black American self
  Not just one little elf who needs some help
Black individuals certainly have to control themselves
  But black people have to control black people as well
As we get rid of agents and spies
  We have to control everything about our lives
That means full control
  Of our religious and educational institutions
    And full control of our economic resolutions
We have to learn to think outside of the square
  To encourage our people to become more aware
Expecting fairness in this system is about as dumb as dope
  Sovereignty is our only useful hope
We don't have any more time for fear and hesitation
  If we want to survive
    We better be about the business of building our own nation

After marching in circles for decades, it has become painfully obvious that we are in great need of a clear vision of the end game. We need to know where we are going. We need to know what we are trying to accomplish and what victories will still leave us without power. A brief anecdote will lead us in this direction. About two decades ago, my mentor set about to teach me the importance of the game of chess. A lot of wisdom came across the table that day. I listened interactively for six hours without a chess board between us. He wanted me to understand the concepts as they relate to life. Long before he talked about starting the game, or even strategies of the game, he trained my focus most importantly on how to end the game. He went over various ways of combining pieces to end the game.

In our previous work, *Elusive Quest for Freedom*, we ended with a discussion of how the game of chess can be understood as directly relevant to our lives. All we have to do is change the pieces on the back row to make them relevant to our situation. For the history and details on each piece, please see the title mentioned above. In this book, we will pick up where we left off. In terms of the struggle for freedom, it has been said that black Americans are still marching in circles. Our actions clearly demonstrate that we do not understand the teachings of my mentor. Through the generations, we are passing the baton of activism without passing instructions on how to win, how to end the game.

The following pages represent more than just a poetic book about freedom. We are making our best effort to be solution oriented. Of course, we will keep marching in circles if we do not know where we are going, if we have no clear vision for the future, if we do not know how to end the game. The first step in marching out of oppression is to clearly define what is necessary for us to survive as a group in ways that cannot be easily reversed. It is important for the framework to involve the biological need for survival as opposed to an emotional want of freedom. We are not going to list a ten-point plan of what we want. We will use the terms necessary for us to survive as a group. While progress in inevitably cyclical, we have to make sure that it is not circular. In other words, we must not allow 180° change to degenerate into 360° change which puts us right back where we started.

Our movements tend to make gains that are nullified by subsequent aggressive policies. We have to win more than Civil Rights. We have to win human rights that enable us to control our own destiny. We cannot allow black leaders to compromise all of our freedoms away. Our leaders are obviously chosen for us in order to sell us out while making it look like progress. We have to learn from history and not continue with this same mistake. Our leaders have to be accountable and have to be fired when they do not serve the needs of the black masses. We know that our adversary is waiting at every turn to deceive us and often uses our own people to do it with promises of great wealth and prestige. As long as we are led by money, we will never get freedom. Who do we think is controlling the money? If we are led by money, then we are led by the people who control the money. We can control our own money which we will discuss later. We have to define freedom for ourselves and not let the concept of freedom be bastardized by the great deceiver.

The second step is to develop strategies that enable us to transition into patterns of greater autonomy leading ultimately toward sovereignty. We do not need hand-outs. We need freedom. In order to achieve this freedom, we have to get back to producing and controlling the things necessary for our basic survival. Decades ago, Elijah Muhammad spoke about food, clothing, and shelter. These needs have not changed, yet our progress in this area has worsened. We let the USDA run black farmers off the farms. Production of clothing has moved to China. And we are still getting 30-year mortgages from white banks to the limits of our income as if this makes sense. We were in a black owned bank one morning opening an account with many other people. While we were waiting, we opened a discussion of building black wealth to all those in the room. No takers. Not one person in the room was interested in any dialogue about coming together financially. Opening an account at the black bank was just a token of concern for another police murder of a black person. We did not even get to tell them about Claud Anderson's *Powernomics* as an economic means to transition to greater autonomy.

Most of us realize that we are in a worse mental condition than we were during the Civil Right Movement. Supposedly, we are better educated. In light of Carter G. Woodson's work, it becomes clear that we are more miseducated, which explains why our mental condition has worsened even in light of having more schooling. We have not listened to Amos Wilson as he told us that the greatest wealth of any people is in their minds. If we cannot envision freedom, if we cannot think of freedom, if we do not really desire to be free, then it makes it impossible to get there. The poems and other writings in this book will speak to this problem. Indeed, this book comes about specifically because of our mental condition. We intend to use repetitive liberation language so that by the time you finish the book, you will have a clear, inculcated understanding of what freedom is for black Americans and why it is imperative for us to follow this course in order to survive.

The third step in this process has to be developed simultaneously with the first two. While oppression is based on aggression, liberation has to be deeply rooted in defense. In order to generate a critical mass of energy, we have to be as assertive in defense as the invader is aggressive in offensive domination. In the rules of chess, white always moves first. He is the aggressor. As this applies to our group circumstance, it does not predestine us to being losers. The invader's aggression can be used against him. We just have to come to grips with the fact that this is not a class game. It is a game of survival and we have no choice but to play black. In fact, the distraction of class stratification is one of the failures of the Civil Rights Movement. It is not our intention to discredit the movement, but it is our intention to learn from its successes and failures.

The class distraction created quite a few wealthy, individualist-oriented black leaders. We cannot move forward with this kind of leadership. Hanging on to the hope of becoming one of the black elite business owners, entertainers, or athletes does not lead to freedom. We have about 40 million black people in this country with about 40 thousand millionaires. That is one-tenth of one percent. It makes no logical sense whatsoever for us to continue down this manipulative path. Anyone with eyes can see the need to work toward survival of the 99.9% of us. Consider Chicago, for example, including billionaires Michael Jordan and Oprah Winfrey. How is it that Chicago still has some of the worst schools in the country? How has the wealth of the black elite affected the liberation of the masses? How did the Mayor get away with closing 54 schools as a response to the striking teachers who won some concessions? They play these same elitist games with the leadership in African countries so that the people never actually achieve freedom. We have to be clear about the end game which is the end of white rule. Here we will start with a series of poems that move us progressively toward understanding the end game.

End Game

The end game cannot be won
  By acting, singing, or manipulating a ball
But if we create a foundation for a solid survival strategy
  We can stop our downward spiraling fall
What do we learn as the goal?
  What is the vision we would like to see unfold?
Are we too distracted by deceit
  To recognize that our vision remains incomplete?
We should be cleaning out the cache of slave files in our minds

Including those which involve our beliefs
Does what we believe
   Give us the best chance of survival in the end?
Did we really think religion was not a part of the game
   That we find ourselves in?
It has many layers, false prophets and soothsayers
   Who can change directions as fast as Gale Sayers
While the big money goes to the preachers
   The entertainers and the ball players
But not to anybody who can help us with direction
   It certainly is not happening by democratic elections
Our resources have to be used toward the end game
   Otherwise conditions improve slightly
     While our impotence remains
Unable to affect lasting change
   Because we cannot call freedom by its real name
We cannot end the game until we can defend ourselves
   Of course every attempt at this is derailed
By a system that would prefer us to be slaving away
   Or rotting away in jail
     Feeling like we've failed
We are still trying to integrate into a capitalist/slave system
   And wondering why we cannot win
We are still losing miserably
   Because we don't understand the situation we're in
Is freedom defined
   By getting along with white people in this place?
Or might freedom depend
   On developing and defending our own space?
We have to ask ourselves the following dichotomous question
Do we want to continue to bend?
   Twisting and stretching like a contortionist
To make sure the invader is rich and happy

Or do we want to win?
Making a way of survival for that group of us whose hair is nappy
If we cannot get past material things
   And start working towards survival as a group
     The point of an end game is moot

Choices of Freedom

Freedom is...
Freedom is being able to do whatever we want to do
   Freedom is deciding to destroy the whole world if we choose to
The water is being polluted causing sickness everywhere
   We are so busy chasing bankrupt dollars
     That we do not even have time to care
Fire is being morbidly abused with bombs made to kill
   Innocent women and children at will
The keepers of the Earth join the deadly forces
   And the madness continues...still
Air pollution reduces the quality of life for humans
   And other living things as well
Our world is being transformed from a place of abundance
   Into a place called hell
The land is being raped of her fertility
   While taxes are charged to her people
The beneficiaries are those who promote religions
   Through war and shrines with steeples
Freedom is...
Freedom is being able to do whatever we want to do
   Freedom is deciding to remain in bondage if we choose to
We are being shackled and confined everywhere in this country
   While we imagine we are spiritually free
     Through Jesus of Nazareth or Muhammad of Saudi
Some are being called successful

In this economic system of opposing design
This system confines us within the steel bars of capitalism
   And is obviously malign
We protect and serve the interest of the ruling class
  As if it makes some logical sense
Our cognitive processes have not been marked to last
    Even Ivy League schools do not bring out our true intelligence
     That is...knowledge of cultural relevance
We are taught how to be European
  So we can become good white people bound in black skin
   All of this is done for us to try to fit in
Freedom is...
Freedom is being able to do whatever we want to do
  Freedom is working to restore harmony if we choose to
Our healing can flow purely
  Like the water of the old Mississippi
We can support Nature's medicines that truly heal our bodies
   That sends a positive resonance to our progeny
Let us defend against Europe's aggression
 In this occupied territory
   As we defend against false narratives and deceptive allegory
This is a melting pot of people
  Who continue to take away our free destiny
   It's getting the best of me
We are already paying for water
  Let us save from pollution our precious winds
We are so caught up in the invader's culture of destruction
  That we do not even see our sins
Let us breathe in the security of an ecology that is fit for later times
  A place that we can call home, a place that is first Divine
Freedom is...
Freedom is being able to do whatever we want to do
  Freedom is deciding to define our identity for ourselves

If we choose to
We assume we are past slavery
   While someone else defines our condition
      Our knowledge of past and present is mostly fiction
We were slaves then Negroes
   Then black then African Americans to boot
While the seed is the beginning
   The trickster has us chasing after roots
Following an imposed identity does not clarify who we are
   Black American people predate the invasion
      Our seed does not come from afar
All living things need a place to be free
   Which causes our struggle to go 'round and 'round
      I pray we will come beyond
Being indifferent, undisciplined, opinionated and individualistic
   So that we will no longer remain bound

Caged bird

I know why the caged bird cries,
   Because it cannot successfully free itself
      No matter how hard it tries
Behind bars and all alone where its only friend is sorrow
   As its hopes, wishes and dreams that it may break free tomorrow
Heartfelt cries for freedom are interpreted as song
   Like old Negro spirituals from times long gone
The bird flaps its wings in vain
   Providing us with one of the clues
That the high pitch melody we hear
   Is really a flightless bird crying the blues

The title of the previous poem was, of course, inspired by Maya Angelou. Although the poem is very short, it speaks to many of the issues that black Americans struggle with. The early part of the poem reminds us of Jesse Jackson and 'keeping hope alive', or of Barak Obama with the 'audacity of hope'. These are false attempts at liberation that leave us without a working definition of freedom. We are left rotting away in a cage. Comfort in a cage is what we hope for. Well, hope is not going to get us to freedom. Old Negro spirituals are not going to get us there either, but it would be encouraging to hear our National Anthem at professional sporting events since most of the players in the NFL and NBA are black. Our clue to the problem is given near the end of the poem. We cannot fly. Even with both parents in the home, we still do not learn how to fly. Our parents teach us how to stay in the cage and get along with white folks. We do not actually learn how to feed ourselves or how to break out of the cage of white rule. We are going to have to rethink our strategies because thus far, our attempts at freedom have been denied.

Freedom Denied

Black freedom is a crime punishable by death
  Genocide in full effect until there is none left
Black freedom is continually denied
  Continuously pushed aside
  Systematically terrorized
Like the rising tide with levee blown
  Remember the 9th ward where there was no love shown
  Black people better get their own
From the top of education, we are criminalized
  As William Bennett unmasked his disguise
See, nothing has changed since the start of the game
  Spinning in circles while things stay the same

Slavery ain't over; they just changed the name
Why is there a war in Afghanistan?
   To create junkies on the corner with dope in their hands
Why is there a war in Iraq?
   Because freedom is denied as the devils won't stop
Disarm the people and then invade
   Beating up old people because they are still slaves
His only crime was coming back
   To the city of New Orleans where he was attacked
Terrorize people out of their own city
   Young or old, they show no pity
We are not qualified to rebuild with government contracts
   But we are fully qualified to be taxed to the max
How long will we continue to complain?
   And allow the slaver to control our brains
Keeping our heads stuck in the sand
   As we continue to invest in the white power plan
     Damn!
We can see no light
   Our intuition tells us that something is not right
But we don't know who to fight
   We don't know how to use our might
We are going to have to boycott
   In order for oppression to stop
We have to organize with self-determination
   And be committed to a black nation
It is only unified that we can stay alive
  And gain the ultimate prize
    FREEDOM

I Dream of Freedom

I dream of freedom

I dream of not having to drive across town
   To work for European invaders
     There has to be something greater
I dream of a time when we are not hunted down and killed
  Like Trayvon Martin
    And found missing on milk cartons
I dream of a time when we are not killed every 36 hours
    When smiling children's faces are not turned sour
As they are harassed and executed by police or police wannabees
  Stop this hot war. Put it on freeze
Freeze right there as you try the psyche game
  Or perpetuate the myth that we are already free in Jesus name
Because I dream of the freedom to define freedom for ourselves
  And I find that equality is not freedom
    As the fight for independence has gone stale
Freedom is not when former slavers
  Allow us to have an equal and fair share of our labor
Freedom is when we have our own
  Flying our own flag on a place we call home
When we don't have to wait on others to decide what we can have
  If we allow the truth to be told
    Freedom is self-control
I dream of being free of oppression
  Domestic and international military aggression
But also,
  I dream of having our own military
    So that we can defend ourselves properly
      Not giving our resources over to a white monopoly
I dream of being able to defend ourselves
  From the invading English colonists after the Revolutionary War
    I have good and bad thoughts about how to even the score
I dream of being able to defend ourselves like Jews in Israel
  After World War II

Since, white revolution is extolled
   I dream of a time when black revolution is acceptable too
I dream of a time when we can be free
   Of the slaver's-imposed religiosity
     When our historical spirituality piques our curiosity
Because it affects how we define freedom today
   As we attempt to rise above the fray
Freedom does not look to a savior of another race
   Truth is right... in your face
Freedom does not promulgate the idea of one human race
   When black people are abused and oppressed all over the place
Freedom takes the blinders off
   While those around me may scoff
I still dream of freedom even when my eyes are closed
     Like John Henrik Clarke, I'll continue to travel this road
I dream of accessible foods that are not genetically modified
   That modifies our genetics and gives us cancer nationwide
I dream of freedom from miseducation
   Unchained from the fantasies of invading nations
I dream of living in harmony with nature
  Without polluting the Earth, Wind and Water
     Without terrorizing Arab people with unprovoked slaughter
Dreams of ending environmental racism and carcinogenic waste
   I time when gradualism is over and we make haste
We make haste to stop the madness of the foreign virulent force
   But be ready for the backlash, of course
I dream of not being called a terrorist
   Because I fight against white supremacy
     Which is lunacy
Against European and Jewish dominance
   Which means military industrial complex
Which manifests in extreme violence
   Because they never seem to be able to come correct

These are the people who kill my dreams
  Bearing witness from the torment I've seen
    These are the people of anti-freedom
But my dreams they can never take
  Because whether fast asleep or wide awake
    I dream of freedom

Unplugged

Are we stuck in a real life Matrix
  Or is some group just playing hate tricks?
Is this the only way things can be done
  Or can we add something to the mix?
The red pill or the blue pill
  The old deal or the new deal
    How can we discern and embrace that which is real?
Everything has become so high tech
  But poor people are still banking on lottery bets
We are still defeated and mistreated
  But nobody is talking about freedom yet
This is obviously why we can get no respect
  One day soon we will all regret
    Not unifying with each other so that our needs can be met
We are divided by television and radio fiction
  Even our miseducation instigates friction
    The medicine for change requires a new prescription
The new medicine is a conscious choice to become unplugged
  Or continue to be drugged and drug through the mud
As long as we live with a predator
  We will be victims of what a predator does
Is this life of oppression just a bad dream?
  Or can we establish our own ways and means?
    And work towards printing our own green

We know the system is lying to us and stealing our souls
  Bent on working us like slaves until we are old
  But if we become unplugged, we can break the mold
We could unplug the radio and unplug the T.V.
  And begin to protect the images that we see
  To discontinue being victims of inferiority
We could unplug our education from public schools
  So that we no longer learn to be over-consuming fools
  Still confined to a polity in which a foreign slaver rules
Somehow we must secure the antidote to our zombie like state
  And begin to dialogue about our fate
  Because we are perishing at an accelerated rate
Perhaps the antidote involves some contemplation
  About the true failure of integration
  And the possibility of becoming our own nation
At a minimum Black Americans must control our seeds
  So that we can provide for our families' future needs
  Without waiting on the military's 'week late' deliveries
Unplug from the system that lulls us to sleep
  Make an unwavering commitment to ethnic unity
  Because only our will, not a pill enables us to become free

We appreciate your indulgence into a long string of poems. The meaning of freedom has become so distorted and confusing that we thought we would approach the problem poetically. We trust that it was varied enough to offer useful interpretations of freedom. We shared the idea that progress is only made if it leads toward the end goal, which we state as the end of white rule of black people. We looked at several poems that should allow us to agree on a definition of freedom. We did not mention much about degrees of freedom, but we will do so in the next chapter and it will be illustrated in a diagram. We just need to continue running the race until we have completed the journey of self-rule. We do not want to fall into the trap of becoming content with how far we have come. There is no need for a party at the first mile of a marathon, especially if the race officials keep changing the starting point. If the new starting point is where we are now, then we have made no progress in the race at all.

There are three steps covered in this section that enable us to move past marching in circles. The first step is to understand our need for group survival. Second is to develop an appropriate strategy. Third is to find a way to defend our strategy. Following our discussion and this section of poems, we would like to share an essay that was written in 2013 for the 50th anniversary of the March on Washington. It also includes poems. Voting was one of the major strategic goals in the early 1960s. We should keep in mind that if politicians are controlled by oppressive moneyed interests, then voting is not a 'compensatory counter racist act' for the masses of poor black people. It is reduced to a symbolic exercise only that makes us feel as if we are part of something democratic. The first step in solving this problem is to establish organizations that bring us candidates who will make sure that our needs are appropriately addressed. Otherwise, there is no efficacy in voting. The following essay entitled, *March Madness* combines the political ideas of freedom and marching and concludes with a political diagram.

"So, you think you found a solution, but it's just another illusion."
-Bob Marley
So Much Trouble in the World

Chapter 2   Marching and Dreaming

Essay: March Madness

In August of 2013, we celebrated the historic March on Washington from fifty years ago. There will certainly be no lack of reflection on the progress or regress of Black American quality of life since that time. Some will cite the larger black middle class to demonstrate that we have moved forward. Some will cite the larger black prison population to demonstrate that we have moved backwards. In this treatise, we will try to deal more with the nature of the problem and the nature of our historic approach to solving the problem. Our analysis will complete the circuit with our perspective on big-picture solutions. In so doing, we will include poems, a short story, a rewrite of Dr. King's, "*I Have a Dream*" speech and a diagram.

At first glance, we see a problem with the nomenclature. This is of great importance because we repeatedly fall prey to the trappings of tricky language, particularly as it relates to legal matters. Not only that, but the language used also creates an idea of the nature of something that may be passed on as an archetype to future generations. The March on Washington can alternatively be referred to as a march on D.C. since there is another place named Washington. This is not a trivial difference in semantics. As a result of our miseducation, the name Washington brings up images of George Washington and the idea of founding fathers. Conversely, the name D.C. stands for the District of Columbia and black people know Columbus as the initiator of genocide in the Americas.

It is not coincidental that this city has a sports team named the Washington Wizards. It is a seat of deception for national and global trickery. Cornell West has referred to this kind of behavior as monstrous mendacity and hyper hypocrisy. The District of Columbia is factually, empirically a district of genocide. The initials D.C. could just as well stand for deceptive con-artists. We find it important to our survival that we teach our children in a way that is relevant to liberation rather than in a way that is relevant to maintaining the status quo, which perpetuates our oppression. It has been said that the most powerful weapon of the oppressor is the mind of the oppressed. In order to overcome this problem, we must teach our children the unadulterated truth. We must teach them to do something about the deceptive con-artists in the district of genocide. If you are reduced to marching, march on D.C.

In dealing with the nature of resistance, we have identified three areas in which we have been historically and currently tricked. These are scripted resistance, diluted resistance and co-opted resistance. Scripted resistance is a top-down approach implemented by brainwashed black leaders who work with the deceptive con-artists in Washington to accomplish three things. First, they enrich themselves with money and positions of authority. Second, they must choose a strategy that makes only superficial changes without upsetting the status quo or power structure. Third, it must be a convincing approach that has the appearance of resistance. Although the miseducated black leaders involved may believe strongly in their activism, this solution is only an illusion. This follows from the Bob Marley quote that began this essay. Yes, we are insinuating that the March on Washington included some aspects of scripted resistance. I am comfortable with the assumption that almost all of the leaders were Christian, yet none chose to demand, like Moses, that Washington D.C. "let my people go." Perhaps a poem will offer some perspective on this.

Let my people go

When, where, why and how
  Let my people go now!
Before we have suffered beyond the point of no return
  When we are satisfied with a luxury ride
    Consumed by the pennies we earn
Let my people go now!
  Before we are all locked away in chains
    Forced to labor in slavery by a different name
Let my people go now!
  Before we have lost all knowledge
    Of how to feed, clothe and heal ourselves
      The last time we had a checkup, we weren't doing so well
Let my people go now!
  Before we forget we are a people with a divine right to freedom
    Before we become so dependent on the oppressor
    We forget that we don't need 'em
Let my people go where?
  To the soil where so many of us originated
    Right here in the Southeastern land
    Where scores of flat-topped pyramids still stand
Let my people go where?
  To the place where we were amalgamated
    From displaced and indigenous people and
The unfortunate inclusion of the rapist himself
    Disguised as a statesman or businessman
Let my people go where?
  To 13% of this land on which to thrive
    We are a unique mix of people with a divine right
    To land on which to survive
Let my people go where?
  To the place of understanding our identity

As a beautifully diverse people of
  Native American, African, Latin American and Asian blood
Where knowledge of self is broad and deep
  Underlying the most powerful freedom movement ever thought of
Let my people go why?
Let my people go on moral grounds
  Show the world that you have some moral clout
    Show the world that you are not the recessive devil
      That Elijah Muhammad wrote about
Why? Let my people go on spiritual grounds
  Because you now know that we are all connected.
    As you continue to terrorize the Global South
      You will soon be affected.
Why? Let my people go because you cannot be free
  While you hold others enslaved
While you project to the world pretentious stories
  Of being noble and brave
Why? Let my people go so that you can experience full humanity
  Your hyper aggressive fear of genetic annihilation
    Is expressing itself as insanity
Let my people go how?
  Through the creativity of our diverse genes
    To finally overcome European and Jewish domination
    Ingenuity unlimited toward building a truly free nation
How? We are going to tell our children about miseducation
  Misinformation and the new Jim Crow
Because it is imperative that they know
  About the agents of repression and Cointelpro
How? We are going to develop an independent mindset
  frame of reference, and worldview
We will not continue to be brainwashed by the state
  And by the media who control what we think and do
Let my people go how?

By any means necessary!

The next topic is diluted resistance. This can occur when the oppressor uses a strategy of playing both sides. One of his tactics is to join your march, defuse your emotions, and dilute your resistance to make it more amenable to his continued domination. Many well-meaning Europeans in the U.S. do this without necessarily being consciously aware of it. They help turn a liberation struggle for human rights into an integration struggle for civil rights. Reflecting on the March on Washington reveals aspects of diluted resistance. As Elijah Muhammad taught, inclusion dilutes the resistance.

There is another very important aspect of dilution. The problem of mass incarceration has another insidious trapping. Even if a person has committed no crime and received no jail sentence, he/she may still have to plea bargain and be left with a felony. In many states a felon cannot vote. So, the civil right of voting that we fought so hard for can be easily diluted by over-policing a certain group (i.e. stop and frisk) and forcing them through a systemic process that will likely charge them with a felony. Since felons have limited, if any voting privileges, voting as a form of resistance is diluted by significantly reducing the number of voters. We will use a couple of poems to convey our thoughts about the efficacy of voting as we have witnessed it since the 1960s.

Vote for freedom!

What Pharaoh did Moses vote for?
  Did he choose to vote?
Or did he choose to break free from the bondage
  Of an unequal yoke?
What did he determine would keep his people afloat
  Freedom or a vote?

Does your vote contribute to emancipation?
  Does your vote build a black nation
Like Cuba with superior healthcare and schools?
  Or, do we continue to get played like fools?
    Where the slave-master continues to rule?
How is the vote doing in Iraq?
  Will this make the madness stop?
Will it stop as a result of their voting?
  Will it stop as a result of our voting?
    I think not
People say, if you don't vote, you don't count
  The U.S. has proven that if you do vote, you don't count
Voting does not stop the tricks that are being played
  It does not ensure that you will be saved
Black candidates must uphold the status quo
  And there we go
Bowing down to the corporations
  As Black Americans continue to suffer without a nation
If we start getting the upper hand, the invader will destroy
  Like the riots and lynching where black progress was left void
As we fight for votes
  Our adversary fights to lock our men in jail
    To make sure that the voting process fails
Get freedom on the agenda with international support
  To give us something worth voting for
    Against the Devil and his cohorts
As an independent nation
  We could have done something about Rwanda or Sudan
    But all our vote does is show submission to the man
Truth be told,
  We need a better plan

Vote for the lesser of two evils?

'Tis the season of the vote hype
I am anticipating the time when
  We will see the light
I perceive that our electoral process
  Is just not right
It locks us into rather than
  Brings us out of our plight
Illusions of freedom allow them
  To totally control our lives
Away from our homes are forced
  The children and our wives
While politicians are still telling
  Us the same lies
And we will never notice anything is wrong
  Until another prophet dies
We have been tricked with illusions of choice
  At the end of the day, we still have no voice
Many people continue to think
  They can change the system
Assuming Uncle Sam will not list them
  As expendable, alive or dead
    On documents that you never read
Can you comprehend what is being said?
  Haven't too many people already bled?
While we win elections and think
  That we are a success
Our lives remain in a total mess
  Efficacy in public programs is less
    But, of course, we cannot get Uncle Sam to confess
I am urging us to contemplate
  And create a brighter day

In which we realize dependency on slavers
  Is not the only way
We do not have to succumb
  To the games they play
We must come together
  And be fully committed to a better way
So that we can implement and defend
  An effective process of our own design
We are not going to march politically down the street
  And get Sam to change his mind
  About how he treats our kind
Neither can we vote him out of his own set up
  Explaining that we have already filled his cup
  And at this point we have just had enough
Rather than lock ourselves into politricking
  Let us work our way out of this systematic rut

    They steal our labor. They steal our land. They steal our dreams. They steal our plans. We're not just talking about profiting from keeping us reduced to convenient excerpts from Dr. King's dream. We are talking about co-opted resistance as it relates to a discussion of civil rights. The tricksters in Washington D.C. actually made more money and gained more power from the Civil Rights movement than blacks did. They co-opted our movement and used it against us while simultaneously using it for their gain. The economic gap widened rather than narrowed, for example. We got black faces in political offices, but only to the extent that they could please the oppressor and sometimes increase the oppression.

    Our current President Barak Obama is also an example of co-opted resistance. His campaign camp co-opted Cynthia McKinney's platform of change emptied it of substance and gave it to us in a way that would not upset the status quo. This is another trick from D.C., the deceptive con-artists. The rhetoric of change was really just a con game to get you to sign on to another eight years of acceptable oppression. This trick passed before our very eyes even after they have played this game in Africa over and over again. President Obama didn't approach the White House and demand that black people are set free. Instead he chose to join the party, which is an unmitigated orgy of oppression and genocide.

The Electoral College choosing a black President effectively legitimizes the system for people of color. It causes us to forget about creating our own system based on our own social and cultural values. Less radically, it causes us to forget about fighting to change the structure of the current system so that it is not inherently racist or classist. Instead, we are encouraged to believe in a system that we had lost faith in since even a black man is allowed to become president of the U.S.A. We have to keep in mind that the political powers across the nation play the race card to their advantage. The Presidency of Obama is a product of scripted resistance carefully managed by speech writers. It is a product of diluted resistance by diluting our desire to come from under the inhumane domination of foreign invaders. As mentioned, it is a product of co-opted resistance by co-opting McKinney's platform of change. We should be skeptical of a top-down approach in general partially because it is so easy to buy off a few leaders at the top of a hierarchical system. A top-down approach is not a solution. It is another illusion. Once the dust of the struggle settles, freedom is denied. We have already shared a poem with this title.

If we understood D.C. as the district of genocide teeming with deceptive con-artists, we would not be so quick to want to join the party. We need not only to deal with the name of the March on Washington, but in the larger context, we also have to deal with the name of the Civil Rights movement. This does damage to our psyche because civil rights are not synonymous with freedom. We cannot call it a freedom movement because we do not have the right to fight for freedom. We have tried to show thus far that any attempt at freedom will be diluted, co-opted and rescript. In order to keep this from happening, we have to uphold a firm definition of freedom. The following discussion will lead us to an understanding of freedom through broadening our context of civil rights to look at the Revolutionary War, World War II and the Civil War which will not be covered in chronological order. We will cover them in spatial order such that it leads to a firm grasp of black liberation.

Our children are taught about the Revolutionary War in primary school. We even have a holiday that reinforces the idea that European invaders deserved independence because they were mistreated by monarchs and by an unjust system. In short, freedom was defined by these invaders as independence. A nation was born from this independence. Similarly, our children are also taught about Jews who were mistreated in Germany. After World War II, Jewish invaders became an independent nation. For them, freedom from oppression meant independence. This independence was the forming of a nation. We are reminded of a Jewish holocaust to demonstrate that they deserved independence.

Our children are taught about the Civil War in the United States without any restitution. Although Black Americans were treated much worse than British Colonists and German Jews, the outcome of the war did not bring us independence. We were not able to form a nation wherein we were able to protect ourselves. We won't digress into a discussion about Liberia since this was set up before the Civil War as a colony. Terrorism against black Americans followed the Civil War, not independence. What our children are left with is the idea that Europeans deserved independence, Jews deserved independence; but Black Americans are not worthy of independence. For us, freedom has not been defined as independence. This is a problem that leaves us defining freedom as Civil Rights. We would like to share a poem on defining the word 'civil' because we think it will be instructive toward understanding the word freedom and the nature of the problem of limiting one's vision to marching for civil rights.

Civil

I would start with the definitions and connotations
  Of what it means to be civil
And try to find out why the solutions to liberation
  Always seem to be such a riddle
Somewhere between slavery and freedom
  We are caught and kept in the middle
While institutional U.S.A.
  Consistently receives a cultural acquittal

What does civil mean and why should we care?
  Perhaps it is relevant because of the excessive burdens we bear
And we have the high-minded expectations
  Of our representation to be fair
    But against a backdrop of domination, civility is rare

Unless you are one of the chosen few selected to emulate
  With whom the reserve pool of the poor cannot truly relate
We never learn the psychological tricks
  As schools continue to indoctrinate
Rather than bringing out who we are
  Which is the real definition of educate

Apparently civil is like Sybil with multiple personalities
  Supported in full by oppressive legalities
    Based on a supremacist philosophy fraught with fallacies
      Is civil like the war on drugs with never ending casualties?

Can civil be defined by Freire, Taylor-Gatto, or Kozol?
  Can it ever be extended to include freedom for us all?
    Or will it allow injustices to accelerate
Leaving us destitute and appalled
  On a self-destructive track until our entire civilization falls?

Civil Rights, bloody nights, 1960's fight
  Cointelpro reduced nationalism
    Tto an almost forgotten historical blight
As the actualization of freedom
  Was pushed further away from our sights
We settled for concessions
  That leaves us mired in the same plight

Civil's schizophrenia makes her change tactics with new names
  We build movements for improvements
    But then our suffering remains the same
Our lives are not valued as we are treated like life is a game
Altruistic teachers do their best
  Yet seldom affect meaningful change

We have never been more than 3/5 citizens of this imperialist state
  Black children herd to the edifice of instruction
    Still distraught about their fate
Freedom never comes to our neighborhoods
  As we are always told to wait
    We have to learn to define the word 'civil' before it's too late

    The recurring theme throughout this paper and in the poems is that after all the pain and struggle; we are left in the same predicament. When we fight for 180° change, we end up getting empty rhetoric with no change at all, or 360° change which brings us back to the same problem. We may win a case and alter a law in the process of fighting for civil rights. The media comes in and magnifies the gain with great publicity. At the same time or soon thereafter several other laws are passed that work against black progress. For example, the war on drugs laws and the war on crime laws and the increased standardized testing mandates came right on the heels of the legal victories of the 1970's. These are clearly warring against the freedom of a dominated race and class. Selective policing and enforcement ensure that a certain group will not advance.

In hindsight we can see that we need to question the effectiveness of the entire Civil Rights struggle. We may need to consider if we have been led by the wrong people and tricked into fighting for the wrong things. In other words, we have been fighting for things that are not actually liberating or are only temporarily useful. The positive energy of the Civil Rights struggle is that it raises awareness about resistance to domination. The potential trouble with this approach is that it remains in the box and profiles a strategy that does not actually work. Let's look at another poem on this topic.

Civil Rights

Civil Rights put a Band-Aid on an open wound
  If we are not careful, all of our black youth will be locked up soon
    As the flowers of justice are suffocated in the concrete jungle
      And never get a chance to bloom
Papa wasn't a rolling stone
  He was just driving while black or walking while black
    When he was attacked
And left on the street to bleed
  Ultimately motivated by the invader's insatiable greed
This is troubling indeed
  Leaving families to grieve

About missing Atlanta children on a milk carton
　Or young black males deprived of a start
　　Because of a bullet through the heart
　　　Like Trayvon Martin
Not to mention the school to prison pipeline
　Of insidious design
　　Making young adult males harder and harder to find
Leaving the black woman all alone
　Trying to create or maintain a home
She is wounded just the same
　Caught up in a loser's game
　　Cloaked in shame
As she is publicly portrayed as a welfare queen
　For political gain
Excuse me ma'am. Excuse me sir. Coming through
　We've got a bleeder
We make the black woman feel
　That if she's not shaking her backside we don't even need her
Open up those triage doors. We have an emergency on our hands
　We're supposed to be fighting for freedom
　　But we're not making any real demands
　　　We're just kicking the can
As it crumples and tumbles further down the road
　Social programs are being cut and creating a heavier load
It doesn't matter whether the can displays a brand
　Of Pepsi or Coke
Because our progress is still stifled by the man
　Who is bringing in the dope
This problem is much deeper than crack or heroin
　It penetrates to the bone marrow when
When high fructose corn syrup is giving us all diabetes
　　And poisonous chemicals abound in the food that they feed us
Young women reduced to being shake dancers

Elder women ending up with breast cancer
As the wound continues to get worse
  Because we have been infected with a curse
We have been infected with the values of the invader
  What self-destruction could be greater?
In times past, we were learning black pride
 But then the infection created a predilection
  For self-hate to thrive
It has been said the greatest tool of the oppressor
 Is the mind of the oppressed
   As we take on his values and think that we're blessed
We have been infected by a deadly virus indeed
 While this open wound continues to bleed
Infecting our spirits, bodies and minds
 Prohibiting the healing of our kind
We cannot join the virus and expect to win
 This is a most deadly sin
We have to get the infection out
 That's really what this poem is all about
Somebody, Ben Carson, come help us to heal
 Because Bill Cosby keeps putting us down
As he berates those in need
 He would lead us to believe
  That the prescription has already been found
Pump more infection into the blood
 As let's see what this does (crazy man)
It's just another program
 For us to continue to be damned
  Without any healing in sight
We get so sold
 On Capitalist goals
  Until we cannot understand wrong from right

At some point, we have to realize
  That we took our eyes of the prize
    And our healing requires that we take up a new fight
Meanwhile...
Open up those triage doors. We've got a bleeder.
  We have an emergency on the gurney
Our vital statistics are not good
  But we can still save the people in the neighborhood
    If we re-evaluate the Black American journey
While some are devalued and dejected
  Understand that we are all connected
    The wound will not heal by covering it up
This is not a Civil Rights tirade
  But recognize that a pale-colored Band-Aid
    Will only keep us stuck in this rut
Our healing depends on liberation
  Which is our ability to build an independent nation
    But we will never see this on any cable TV station
We have to search deep inside
  To comprehend why we're alive
    And get re-focused on the prize
Only liberation can repair the wounds of slavery
  To the degree with which we accomplish this feat
    Will our healing be complete

The main reason we find that a strategy limited to civil rights remains in the box is because the goal of this strategy is not freedom. Social change is not freedom. Because you ameliorate someone's conditions does not mean that you have set him or her free or allowed them self-determination that enables freedom to manifest. Civil rights and social changes unquestionably help to alleviate inhumane conditions, but they do not set us on a path toward self-reliance, independence or full human expression. The problem is that the same power structure remains intact. As a result, civil liberties can easily be rolled back, and social safety nets can be cut. Laws are passed to keep the masses of oppressed people from ever benefitting from civil changes.

It becomes clear that when we consider the gains from any movement, we must also consider the backlash of repression. The net gains may actually be negative. It is necessary to look at the big picture. The topic of civil struggle, for example, allows for an easy comparison of the Civil War and the Civil Rights movement. It is important for children to see that overt repression followed the Civil War and covert repression followed the Civil Rights movement. We will never make any genuine progress as long as we allow our children to be brainwashed by the state. Upon reaching adulthood, they will not understand who we are and what our relationship is to the foreign, invading, occupying, imperialist force that we are dealing with. We will just keep leading them in circles. Here we are inserting a recent poem on this topic, but the essay written in 2013 ends with a political diagram.

Marching in circles

There is no value in marching in circles
　Our feet are getting blisters and toes turning purple
Led by clergy who are trained by the adversary of our march
　We are doomed from the start
　　We have been thoroughly deceived by the psychological part
So, we have only been led deeper into the bowels
　Of the same system
Where is the love for our murdered children?
　Do we really miss them?
Marching is not an awareness rally
　Where people are giving donations and taking tally
Marching is for the strategic goal of advancing

Then the question becomes, what are we advancing?
Are we advancing the goal of self-control?
  Or still using the tactics of old?
Still begging for justice in a foreign invader's club?
  Hoping and praying that they might show us some love
We are still marching in circles
  As our feet get blisters and toes turn purple
We bring awareness to our plight
  But without any binding demands
We cannot defend any demands
  Because we have no land on which to take a real stand
Taney wrote that blacks "had no rights
  Which the white man was bound to respect..."
    We know that we are owed an unpayable debt
But, when we march to the capitol
  What are we really trying to collect?
We have to start marching into our own productivity
 That we can demand respect for
    We have to control the keys and the locks to opportunity's doors
Think about why we are asking a foreign invader for rights?
  While we are working hard all day and can't sleep at night
We must assert control over our own destiny and economy
  It need not be a secret that this requires autonomy
How are we expected to control our youth
  When we cannot control our youth?
We don't control the schools
  We don't control the rules
We don't control the music, the film, the sports, or social media
  We don't control the information in Wikipedia
    Or the Encyclopedia
Yet, we are 40 million black people with a divine right to self-rule
  The New Jewel Movement has to be able to protect the Jewel [1]
Begging for rights in a former and current slave system

Is not a solution
   It is evidence of mental pollution
What actually happens is dissolution
   Regardless of how well-intentioned our contribution
A foreign invader controls our children's minds
   The overwhelming amount of time
Whether they are outside or inside the home
   From television, to music, to cell phones
Like a thief in the night, the virus comes in
   Sordid, morbid grim reaper with a grin
And then we know we are sick
   Because we start marching in circles
     Feet getting blisters and toes turning purple
How can we claim to love our children
   And yet lock them into a system
     That murders them with unceasing regularity?
The fact that we cannot defend ourselves
   Is the main driver behind the disparity
Invade and enslave
   That's the way our adversary behaves
Then we fight back by endless marching in circles
   By the time we have finished the circle
They have already found a way around our demands
   So, our bid for survival has to be backed up
     By a comprehensive freedom plan
     Otherwise, we are building our homes on quick sand
Then we wonder why we are falling deeper and deeper
   Into a sunken place
     We are the ones without land, so it's mostly just our race
We don't even realize we have to be in the race for resources
   Our children may not need cows and horses
But they still need land upon which to survive
   A place where we make the rules that enables us to thrive

Then we can march outward from our base
  Filled with meaningful pride in our race
Because we control the resources where we live
  As well as our children
    Protecting them from people and mindsets that kill them
Rather than marching in circles to beg for respect
  We have to march in our ability to build
    And in defense of our ability to protect

[1] The New Joint Endeavor for Welfare, Education, and Liberation, or New JEWEL Movement (NJM). Political party in Grenada led by Maurice Bishop

Let's take in a short story in which our terms of discussion are personified. It should make for palatable transition from a Civil Rights struggle to a freedom struggle.

Short Story: Freedom's family

I caught a glimpse of Freedom the other day. She was up on Resistance Street. You know, over towards Peace Ave. and Harmony Blvd. Yeah, she was down there talking about building a Nation and stuff like that. Of course, she was by herself. Nobody really paid her any attention. Some Muslim brothers walked by, but they did not say anything because she was not covered up from head to toe. Some Christian brothers walked by. They did not bother with her because she did not have any money to pay her tithes. Some intellectual brothers walked by but they rationalized that she did not even exist. The sisters envied her beauty and strength but considered her a primitive thing of the past.

Freedom tried to talk with the common people. They did not want to hear it because she was not talking about money. She tried to move into leadership. She even ran for office but did not

get any votes. In fact, her name never made it on the ballot. Being alienated and misunderstood, Freedom was finding it increasingly difficult to keep hope alive. She was left isolated, all alone near the corner of Peace and Harmony. Our cousin Wisdom, used to hang out over there too, but he was run out of town a long time ago. We don't even hear from him anymore.

Freedom wandered around like the Buddha and then the folks picked her up for loitering. They treated her like a junkie. She was homeless, but she was clean. They sent the head man after her, Mr. Status Quo himself. It wasn't pretty because you know Freedom has a lot of fight in her. She was born and raised over there on Resistance Street. Regrettably, there was no one there to help her. She didn't have a following. She had no support at all. The crowd was quiet and fearful as she went away, again.

She saw her sister in lock down, who was doing triple life. Her name is Unity. It seems like she ain't never getting out. We would need Johnny Cochran and Thurgood Marshall to rise from the dead to get her out. Even though she was falsely accused, DNA evidence doesn't seem to be working in her favor. It certainly did not lead Oprah to put any money on her books. Anyway, Freedom had become nearly despondent when she saw her sister Unity's condition. Freedom knew Unity had been locked up for a long time; but she looked like she had been tortured and abused. So, Freedom wanted to come up with a plan to get them both out.

Now, she dared not tell Unity about our other sister. It would have just taken her over the edge. Not long after she got locked up, our other sister got involved with Status Quo. You have to remember, Status Quo is a dangerous man. He is merciless against any threats to his domination. He even locked up our brother, Self-Reliance because he was hanging out with a group of homies up on Liberation Trail, led by Independent Thinker. They said it was gang related. Everybody in the neighborhood was afraid of Independent Thinker, including Status Quo but they couldn't lock him down. I think it's Status Quo's fear that makes him so slick and deadly. He even tried to kill our Mother. Her name is Nature.

Yeah, man it's true. He even tried to kill Mother Nature. He and his uncle raped her and are holding her hostage right now. So, we are trying to save her too. I couldn't tell Unity what was happening to our Mother. She had already fallen apart. Our other sister didn't realize what was going on because she wasn't too bright. She married Status Quo not long after Unity went to jail. This sister's name is Civil Rights. They moved out to the suburbs on Trick'em Court. That's where they operate from. My Mother, remember Mother Nature, thought somebody had taken her head off and replaced it with a cinder block. We were certain she had lost her mind when she married Status Quo.

We have been getting Freedom out of lock down every few decades. But it is getting harder and harder to get Freedom out each time. She has been up for parole since the 1960s and she cannot even get a public defender. That's right. The public won't defend her. The people act like she is dead and gone. They will not run her story on the radio or on the television. They do not have to give her any justice since there is no one to hold them accountable. I'm telling you since Status Quo married into the family, it has been nothing but trouble.

My Mother had six children, three boys and three girls. Two of the girls are locked up, Freedom and Unity. And Civil Rights married Status Quo. Our brother Self-Reliance is in a maximum-security prison. Then there is me. I am telling the story. My name is Mystery. You have probably never seen me. I hang out up on Meditation Place. It is uptown, across the bridge. We have one brother left who went overseas to Africa. If we could get him to come back, it would make a world of difference. His name is Organize. He left the country when Civil Rights married Status Quo. That was just after Unity got locked up and sentenced to triple life. It was too much for Organize to bear, so he went overseas.

The word down on Peace Ave. and Harmony Blvd. is that Organize is coming back. Yeah Jack. They say he is even better than Johnny Cochran and Thurgood Marshall. They say he's got the goods to get Freedom and Unity out. And if that happens, they will not be able to hold Self-Reliance any longer. They are all being held on trumped up charges you know. As quiet as it's kept, everybody was mad about Civil Rights, but not really surprised. You see, she had a different father. Her father's name was Uncle Sam. Yeah, you know him, the rapist himself.

So, Civil Rights was illegitimate you see. We gave her all the love we could; but she never could get right. Uncle Sam had raped our Mother. That is where Civil Rights came from. We just thought maybe she was bi-polar or something, until we got older and Mother Nature told us the truth. Anyway, we are talking to Organize right now. We are trying to get him to come back home and hook up with our cousin, Knowledge of Self. If we just give them some support, I am sure they can help free the family. I am looking forward to it and I hope you are too. Well, I am heading back up Resistance St. on my way to Meditation Place. I will catch you all next time at the intersection of Peace and Harmony. One love.

The purpose of our thesis is beyond the scope of civil rights. Our survival depends on a struggle for human rights, which always means control of land. If we solve the human rights problem, then we will no longer have a problem with a foreign invader allowing us to have equal civil rights. The freedom struggle will allow us to express our full humanity. Toward this end, we need to define the word freedom. A definition of freedom will also make clear what freedom is not. Emancipation from chattel slavery is not freedom. If you unchain a dog that is kept in your yard, this does not make him free. Social change is not freedom either. We explained this as amelioration, not liberation. As a rhetorical example of how to change our mindset from one of civil rights to one of freedom, we have taken an approach that may seem sacrilegious to some readers. We have re-written Dr. King's *I Have a Dream* speech. Since we cannot effectively sleepwalk through life, we have entitled it, *Waking Up From the Dream*. It departs from the current dream-keeping, scripted resistance that builds on convenient parts of King's speech.

Speech: Waking Up from the Dream

It has been 150 years since an invading European, in whose symbolic shadow we remain oppressed, signed the Emancipation Proclamation. This unlawful decree came as a great trick from the Washington Wizards, who hold as their greatest symbol the torch of injustice, called Liberty. Lincoln claimed to bring hope to those bound in the Confederate States of America, in which he had no jurisdiction. The proclamation came as a new beginning and gave rise to new terrorist groups that would try to ensure that blacks in America would never be free. Fifty years after the March on Washington, we must face the tragic fact that Black Americans are still not free.

Fifty years later, the lives of Black Americans are still embarrassingly crippled by the shackles of economic exploitation and still bound by the chains of landlessness. Fifty years later, Black Americans remain without political autonomy and still belong to the same system, yoked to the same capitalism that enslaved us, victims of the same heinous crimes.

So, I am waking us up from the dream to expose a degenerating condition. I am exposing these truths because our nation's capital has tricked us. The architects of this republic copied the words of its constitution from Indigenous Americans, who proved the ways of liberty and justice. It has become obvious that these words were never in the hearts of the plagiarist authors of liberty, who had slaves in their backyards.

The tricks unfold like unending curtains in the dynamic saga of life. Behind the veil, there are many hidden deceptions, such as the Declaration of Independence. This document and ideology is an impossible pill to swallow for America's perpetually oppressed people. There has been no independence for America's indigenous or displaced people of color. We refuse to believe that we cannot be a free and independent people. We refuse to believe that we cannot legitimately Declare our Independence.

So we declare that our survival depends on self-rule. It is clear that we have been treated far worse than the invading European colonists who declared independence. It is time that we demand the reality of true freedom and sovereign justice. We must remind the dominant culture that we are long overdue. This is no time to continue with the mind-altering path of euro centrism. For this interim period has allowed our repressive government to push debilitating drugs deep into our communities. The resulting plague has left our social fabric torn and tattered, exposed to further damage from the weathering of trickery and eroding legislation.

It is a great mistake for this nation to deny Black Americans the self-determination and Nationalism that we have a human right to pursue. This immobilizing winter of our legitimate discontent will not pass until there is a renewing spring of freedom and independence. It is a great mistake to assume that Black Americans are powerless and without solidarity. Those who assume we have allowed assassinations and tortuous crimes to be swept under the rug will have a rude awakening. We have forgiven but not forgotten. We know those who forget their history are doomed to repeat the same mistakes. There will be neither rest nor tranquility in the United States until her people of color have finally achieved independence.

The undermining storms of resistance will continue to weaken the strength of this nation until the new day of justice emerges with freedom. Let it not be washed from our minds that Dr. King said, "injustice anywhere is a threat to justice everywhere." We realize now that we must struggle for justice through independence. There is no freedom without political autonomy. There is no freedom without economic control. Any living thing in a healthy mind desires to be free.

We must conduct our struggle, however, with unconquerable unity and a well-defined understanding of freedom. We must not allow our creative movements to be dismantled or co-opted by covert tricks of repression. Again, and again we must rise to the celestial heights of meeting subliminal coercion with foresight and preparedness. Survivors must resist and defend, but violence should be avoided. It is counterproductive to get into an arms race with the world's most vicious killer. No one in the history of the world has killed like the invading Europeans in America. Manifest Destiny is the worst genocidal aggression known to man. Even Dr. King recognized white America as the greatest purveyor of violence in the world during his time.

As we look back through the dark and painful veil of the 1860's and see also through the quicksand of confusion in the 1960's, we begin to recognize that Emancipation was a trick and that Integration was also boiled in the cauldron of injustice. Integration has tied their destiny to ours such that their freedom depends inextricably on our bondage. Brothers and sisters, we have to come together like kindling in a fire and re-ignite the struggle.

Though we have become divisively conquerable, we must not give up hope in solidarity. We cannot walk alone. And as we walk, we must remember our failures from previous movements. We must protect our enlightened ones and not let assassinations destroy the movement. Black Americans have to be like a many-headed dragon. I challenge those who assume integration has already made us free to show us the political autonomy, to show the economic control, to show the land on which our flag flies. The venomous lies of liberty continue to poison our minds until the rivers of freedom have created a path of self-reliance, pouring into an ocean of independence.

This land will never be seen as a place of freedom until people of color are free. We are the people who did not voluntarily choose this position. But, this nation answers the call of freedom with torture, terrorism, infiltration and destruction. We cannot let U.S. terrorism control us with fear. Continue to work with the faith that wickedness will not prevail in the end. It has its time. It has its cycle. And that time is coming to a fast approaching end. The terrorism of the 1960's and the bomb on Move in the 1980's have deterred us from fighting. It has caused us to turn our backs on the struggle. But as Fredrick Douglas said, "If there is no struggle, there is no progress...power concedes nothing without a demand."

Come from the southeastern farms of our Grandparents. Come from the slums and ghettos of our northern escape routes. Come from our western illusions of grandeur. Come together with the confidence that if we continue to brave the dangers of taking a stand, our situation will eventually be changed. Recognize that separate but equal was a lie. Integrated and equal was a lie. Let us stop chasing illusory dreams of equality. I write to you today, my friends, that in spite of the difficulties and frustrations of the moment, we can wake up from the dream. We can wake up from the dream and see that we are perpetual second-class citizens.

Wake up from the dream this day and recognize the true meaning of freedom, not the pseudo-freedom hypocritically penned in this nation's creed. This nation was born from stealing, killing and destroying. Is that what we call freedom? Wake up from the dream Atlanta, Georgia and realize that former slave owners still hold us in bondage. Wake up from the dream that white people in Mississippi will act like anything other than white people in Mississippi. Wake up and realize as Dr. William White joked, "A leopard don't change him spots." We need to wake up from the dream today.

I pray that we will be able to see beyond the wickedness and trickery that hold our minds and lives in bondage. Wake up and know that in order to be free, we must control our own food, clothing and shelter. I pray that we will begin to define freedom for ourselves so that the healing process can begin. With renewed minds, we will begin to see that our spirituality was tortured out of us and was replaced with the invader's empty view of God. With this understanding, we will be able to transform the jangling discords of our divided people into a beautiful harmony of unity. With this faith, we can begin to sever dependent connections to the slave-master and his culture of bondage for us.

This will be the day when we will have a country fit for our National Anthem, "Lift every voice and sing." America's occupying Europeans must eventually let people of color go. So, let freedom ring from the negative stereotypical images of Hollywood. Let freedom ring from the killing machine at the Pentagon. Let freedom ring from the government agencies that push drugs into our communities. Let freedom ring from the psychological warfare unit that seeks to destroy us. Let freedom ring from the COINTELPRO initiatives that persist to this day. Let freedom ring.

When we let freedom ring, when we begin to take charge of our freedom instead of asking for it, we are no longer dreaming. When we stop expecting blood suckers to act like corn eaters, we are no longer dreaming. When we stop dreaming, when we finally wake up, we will be able to join hands and resound the words of that old Black American spiritual, "Free at last! Free at last! Thank God Almighty, we are free at last!"

We would like to clear up something else as we try to offer a working definition of freedom. Self-determination does not necessarily lead to freedom. This depends on how internalized the slave-mentality is. If a person or group is in the pet stage of slavery, then they do not want to be free and do not know how to be free. They just want to be treated better. This is what they determine. Ultimately the simplest way we can describe individual and collective freedom is as self-control. If we do not control our political process, then we are not free. If we do not control our economic paradigm, then we are not free. If we do not control our educational content, then we are not free. If we do not control the terms of trade, then we are not free. If we do not print our own money, then we are not free. If we do not design and control our own justice system, then we are not free. If we cannot protect ourselves, then we are not free. If we do not have food sovereignty, then we are not free. If we cannot take charge of our own healing, then we are not free.

The nature of the problem has to do with being able to define freedom. We have to know beyond the shadow of a doubt that integration is not freedom. And we should not be ashamed of not wanting to continue being dominated by a foreign invader. We do not need to be timid about the issue out of fear that we might upset the status quo or upset the wrong Euro-Jewish invaders. We have a human right to collective freedom. We have a human right to design our own system. If freedom is defined for Europeans as sovereignty, then it also applies to us. If freedom is defined as sovereignty for Jews, then it also applies to us. One of the greatest tricks played on our minds is to convince us that we are already free. This is what happens as we are taught the Emancipation Proclamation in school. Because we are no longer someone's property does not mean that we are free. Freedom would not have allowed for Ku Klux Klan terrorism. Freedom would not have allowed for Jim Crow laws.

The North was dominated by what Dr. Frances Cress Welsing calls a system of Racism (White Supremacy) and so was the South. Whether blacks sided with the ideology of the North or South, they would not be freed of oppression. The question of the Civil War was which side would dominate blacks, not which side would free blacks. It was a question of how blacks would be oppressed, not whether blacks would be oppressed. Abraham Lincoln changed the way in which blacks were dominated. He did nothing to stop the domination itself. Even when we learn of black abolitionists, we are kept in the box. We learn that Harriet Tubman took people to freedom. No such thing occurred. As we have mentioned, amelioration is not freedom. Harriet Tubman took slaves to better conditions. She did not free them from slavery. It can be argued that we are still slaves to a large degree. Enjoy a poem on this topic.

Save More

Harriet Tubman was unquestionably brave
  But she is getting pimped by history

From metal chains to mental chains
  The freedom game clouds our brains
    While liberation is still a mystery
Deep inside, we all know the truth
  Wealth is built by some, yet freedom still hasn't come
    Even though Harriet Tubman is taught
      To every generation of our youth
She took people to better conditions by helping them to run away
 I Have a Dream by Dr. Martin Luther King
    Explained in no uncertain terms that we are still not free today
But Harriet Tubman left us with some words
  To help us make sense of the struggle
Unfortunately, history is a bore that many ignore
    So we have never overcome this crippling trouble
She said she could have saved more if they knew they were slaves
  Stuck in a rut with no fire in their gut
    We are still in the same bind these days
Now, I could save more if we knew we were slaves
  From modern day slavery or wage slavery
    Still bound to the same system, selling ourselves to get paid
We have slick talking figure heads pretending to call the shots
  Selling us out, casting doubt
    About who is really on the top
Having a few black leaders doesn't mean that we're free
  Who do they work for? Do they really help the poor?
    These are the same old tricks that we still can't see
1865 was not the end of slavery; it was the beginning
  Culturally acclimated, politically dominated
    Whether North or South, black people weren't winning
Because they didn't take the chains off until they had full control
  Broken and abused, completely confused
    We remained fully dominated in body and soul
They gave us Jesus to make us feel freed

Made us meek, turned the other cheek
  While most didn't question whether we were being deceived
If the Civil War really freed black folks
  Explain our plight and the 1960's fight
    The invaders are still parasites and we're still the host
We have not emerged from slavery to a post-racial state
  Continued impropriety, from the top of our society
    Making superficial changes that only placate, but never liberate
I could save more if we knew we were slaves
  Some serious dedication and introspective contemplation
    Will give us the gall for us all to change our ways
From exploiting each other to developing unity
  Creating our own culture, apart from the vulture
    Starting with growing food in our own communities
We need to think more deeply about what freedom requires
  Taught by the invader, thinking his culture is greater
    We lost sight of independence from the empire
The aggression of oppression will never cease
  Tricked by the identity game, believing we're all the same
    While we are still being murdered by security guards and police
Civil Rights was a watered-down joke
  And they are taking it all back
Controlling our movements and what we think are improvements
  Psychology is covertly used in a full-scale attack
Do we know what happened to the Quitman-10?
  They got elected, and then got ejected
    So the same political domination happened all over again
Understanding is becoming inaccessible
  For our necessary education
With our minds in check and finances in debt
  Are we even working towards liberation?
Beneath the surface is where the real difference is made
  By people with vision who are willing to listen

I could save more if we knew we were slaves

The fact is that we are still slaves and we have found over the last 50 years that integration is not a solution to slavery. Joining in the party to steal Indigenous American wealth is not a solution to slavery. Joining the U.S. military to rob other countries of their wealth is not a solution to slavery. John Henrick Clarke told us many years ago that we needed to focus on nation building skills. Since that time, we have actually gone backwards. We are losing our farmers, engineers, doctors, etc. Lamentably, we are still following in the self-destructive footsteps of the foreign invader. We will never fight for freedom if we don't develop a mindset of freedom. This writing is designed not only to share a perspective on the nature of the problem, but also to help us develop a liberating mindset to enhance our ability to survive and help us think about developing a "never again" strategy. Without a never again strategy, we have not achieved freedom.

It has been said that we should just try to make the system work for us. This falls in line with a Civil Rights, integration, and non-threatening kind of strategy. This approach has two major problems. First, we essentially mentioned in the previous paragraph that joining in the systemic stealing, killing and destroying is a bad idea. It is devilish, unethical and destructive. Second our current system is unsustainable. We have been lulled to sleep during the Industrial Revolution. We are destroying the entire planet for the sake of European and Jewish domination. It is not wise for us to try to emulate this behavior. We cannot make the system work for us. We have to design an entirely different system. And we will have to become a sovereign nation in the process of creating a new system. We heard many years ago that you cannot make chicken soup out of chicken poop. Allow us to share a poem with this title.

Chicken Poop

We cannot make chicken soup out of chicken poop
  Trying to make honest money out of stolen loot
As we behold an ugly duckling
  While thinking that we have a golden goose
You might have fool's gold at best
  With U.S. financial poop in trillions of debt
    And the sad thing is…we haven't even caught on yet
More jobs with wage slavery is not a solution
  It's more of the same, which is lame while we continue to remain
    Without independent institutions
      You want things to get better, but what is your contribution?
When we have finally worked our way or voted our way to the top
  Take a closer look at what we have and what we have not
    We won't have a pot to piss in because
      Chinese bond holders will be claiming our lot
The super wealthy have sold the country
  And are running away with the cash
Leaving us in an economic cesspool, spiraling downward fast
  And this is nothing new. They have done it in the past
But, before they relinquish control, they might give us AIDS
  Like it happened in South Africa when apartheid began to fade
  Chicken poop with bombs, guns and machete blades
When the system controls our minds, we are lost in the sauce
  Just when we have worked hard and think we have paid the cost
    Owning our own companies so that we can be the boss
We will inherit a country that is completely bankrupt
  With new political faces that are still inept and corrupt
While police maintain the status quo
  And jam night sticks up our butts
We will be left with a capitalist system
  That never worked in the first place

We will be left with greed, fighting over cheese
   Still stuck in a rat race
     We like to ignore the facts because we are a sad case
They will use all our resources and then return home
  We will be paying the world back
    Even though we didn't get the loans
They have taken all the meat from the soup
  And left us the dry bones
So, stop joining in the one-sided games they play
  And open your minds to hear what I have to say
    Stop fighting to get into a system that hates us anyway
Don't fight to get in. Fight to get out of this bind
   Fight for independence, to create a system of our own design
   Fight to gain control of our children's minds
Enough with the blind obedience
  We must solve this problem with expedience
   A healthy soup must start with new ingredients
I am talking about liberation in case you do not understand
 I am talking about true freedom right here in this land
You may not believe that we can achieve it
  But I know that we can
I am not talking about hooking up with the murdering thieves
  In Washington D.C.
This is about self-determination
  So that we can finally become free
    Where our children can actually learn to be all they can be
Chicken poop has our wills trapped in mire
  And our minds held back
From the possibilities of true freedom under constant attack
   But the reality is, there are no nation building skills that we lack
So, we can exercise our human right to be free from oppression
  If we organize to be unified in a stand against aggression
The use of new ingredients

Means we have to change our direction
We can put our energy into building an independent nation
  And stop wasting time with the deceptive illusion of integration
  All we need is the will, the commitment and dedication
To get out of a downward spiraling system
  with irrational, circular loops
Toxic assets were brought to light
  So we should no longer be duped
    Our survival requires us to realize that…
      We cannot make chicken soup out of chicken poop

So, the solution is…

Independent Institutions

Because we are not included in the constitution,
  We must develop our own solutions
    With a committed return to independent institutions
A good start is local food production
  Making sure everyone is employed
    Taking care of our own by filling in the void
We need land with food sovereignty including water rights
  To develop realistic goals for overcoming our plight
Like the speeches of Malcolm X that are poignant and legendary
  We have to defend our independent processes
    By any means necessary
The oppressor may not be wise, but he is quite cunning
  Still we can liberate ourselves from genocide
    If we stop using their monies
That's right. I said it. We have to create our own cash
  If we don't control our own exchange, our freedom won't last
Many of you will assume that this cannot be done
  Hear this! Stop praying for drama and let's get this battle won

We have black economists, banks, programmers and ingenuity
   With the wherewithal to create wealth
     All you have to do is honestly believe in yourself
If we believe in freedom, the godliness of unity
   Will provide for our needs
We will feed our minds and bodies nutritiously
   And wisely save our seeds
A troubling issue to overcome is when belief is mistaken for truth
   Our liberation can be thwarted
     By teaching foreign religion to our youth
We don't come from the popular but volatile Middle East
   So why should we need these religions to find our peace?
In truth, these religions have not made us free
   We have our own ancestral stories
     That are better rooted in reality
We are mis-educated by religion and schooling
   By cunning and subliminal psychological tooling
The solution is to rise up in spirit and in mind
   By learning the laws of Nature and letting our lights shine
Not by fighting with the darkness
  But by sharing our light
   By embracing Nature's rules with all of our might
Enabling us to break free from suicidal cultural congruence
   And govern ourselves to the exclusion of external influence
As we stop playing a losing capitalist game
   And falling for empty rhetoric of change
Let's stop training the children to be for sale
   And start healing our people until we are well
We must defend our liberation process in the best way we can
   With or without leaders, we have to follow a strategic plan
Because we have long since known the perennial solution
   Is building and maintaining independent institutions

In the final analysis God has blessed the child who has his own. This is another old saying that is quite relevant here. Many people will argue that we cannot have our own country in this land because the dominant culture will not let us. With this mindset, we have affirmed their God complex. Additionally, we have internalized an inferiority complex that interprets European and Jewish domination as impossible to defeat. We assume they are greater than God. As a result, we decide to join them on their destructive crusade against the Earth and her children. European culture was destructive long before the America's were invaded. As part of developing a liberating mindset, we must understand clearly that Europeans and Jews, whom we call white people, are foreign invaders. This is something we should never forget. This is not their land. They are not Americans. They are unambiguously Europeans wherever they may be found. Then we are left with the problem of black Americans being African as if that is the only part of our being that matters and is worthy of research. It disconnects us from the land where we live. This is a different scenario, however. When Europeans are mixed, the children are put with another racial group. This leaves Europeans as Europeans. Therefore, wherever they are, they are still Europeans. They are a fairly homogenous group of non-Americans.

On the other hand, Black Americans are of mixed racial heritage. We have some African, but also Native American, Mexican, European, Indian and Asian in our blood to include Chinese, Vietnamese, Korean, and Filipino. The Americas is the only place in the world where you find that mix. Therefore, we are Indigenous to this land. We come from here. Our mixed group of people is only part African. We are Black American with some African heritage, but also several other groups affect our heritage. This is a topic for an entire book. Suffice it to say that we are an indigenous people of America and we have a divine right and human right to survival as an independent nation right here in this land. For those naysayers who think we cannot achieve it, consider that we have not achieved equality either, but we keep fighting for it. What we are saying is that if we are going to fight for something, we may as well fight for something that is worth fighting for. Let us fight for something that will enable us to develop a "never again" strategy. We cannot do that from a position of someone else telling us what rights we can have, even if they offer us equal rights temporarily to keep us in the system. We will have to stop rejecting freedom in favor of the status quo if we want our children to have a place to survive.

Rejecting freedom

We are not resisting oppression, we are resisting freedom
 Obviously, this is self-destructive, but what is the reason?
Is it a herding instinct that causes us to follow?
 Because if we don't fight the power today
  We will never be free tomorrow
Who are the pied pipers leading us astray?
 Clouding our minds so that we cannot find our own way
Teaching us that our culture is inferior to Europeans and Jews
 It's not news that we are confused, abused, and singing the blues
  But why do we reject information that we can use?
Besides the herding instinct, there is a problem with inception
 Which is the ultimate deception
The foreign invader has placed in our minds
 The idea that we should never attempt to save our kind
After torture and terror for hundreds of years
 We harbor paralyzing mental and spiritual fears
That keeps us from waking up and coming around
 As we remain content
  With murder, incarceration, and dumbing us down
Hiding truth so that it can hardly be found
 Yet we won't stop to get our feet on solid ground

We are afraid to look at Mother Nature
  Because the invader has chains on our brains
We are locked into a box
  Wherein the power structure stays the same
At the invader's insistence
  We typically end up with scripted resistance
We can easily predict what the end result will be
  Wealthy blacks will be placated and none of us will be free
Unfortunately, we have been programmed
  To believe that freedom doesn't pay
    And we would have to sacrifice too much to save the day
The triple problem is that
  We are too ignorant, too lazy, or too afraid to fight
So we follow what the oppressor prescribes
  And focus on Civil Rights
But even when we feel like we are living large
  Our lives are still dominated by the demons in charge
They pay us money from the lives and resources that they stole
  What would help us to actualize our role
Is to realize that freedom is self-control
  Only an independent nation could make us whole
Meanwhile, we are taught that slave teachings are salvation
  To keep us from understanding liberation
Sometimes I wonder what's the use
  We will never become free while we continue to reject truth

A large part of the purpose of this book is to enable us to establish truth from falsehoods, reality from delusion. We do not seem to be clear on the truth about our situation. We erroneously believe that wealth will make us free, which causes us to emulate the invader's capitalist culture of destruction and bondage. This is not only the result of seeds planted in our minds early in life because the seeds of destruction are planted every time we go to school or to work or turn on anything electronic. As mentioned in the previous poem, we have to be concerned with inception. This logical dynamic question whether we are actually thinking for ourselves. Clearly, we are not. There was an interesting movie on this topic entitled, *Inception* (2010). If you are unfamiliar with the concept, then do something constructive with your electronic device and watch the movie. Rather than allowing ourselves to be programmed for servitude, we can choose to program ourselves for self-control. In other words, we have to take control of our own inputs that determine what we think and how we think. Only then can we be confident that we are thinking for ourselves. Obviously, this is not the path of least resistance. It will take some effort. The reader may begin this part of the journey with the next poem.

Inception

How do we know if our desires come from our hearts or heads?
  From our own creativity or an external source instead?
Who plants the seeds of thought in our minds?
  And who makes truth so hard to find?
Desires can be fed into our minds like advertisement
    Full of white supremacy and slave requirements
Thoughts that are not our own
  Thoughts that destroy our homes
    Thoughts that make us feel alone
Inklings that slip under the radar of our awareness
  To remove the possibility of equality and fairness
Of course, life is not fair
  But our society is based on profit, the opposite of care
The yearning of our will ignites a burning fire
  Giving energy to our progressive desires
But then our future is stolen by the vicious empire
  Barred from producing our desires, we become buyers
Consuming not only material things, but also information
  Resulting from the propaganda that makes up our miseducation

The greedy elite control the land and our brains
  The terror of violence and poverty
    Makes us afraid of systemic change
Most people are drinking the Kool-Aid, Jim Jones style
  If you don't drink from the fountain of illusions
    Then they have you on file
The desires of the masses are manufactured by the few who profit
  When they can control your thinking, they can get to your wallet
So, we can desire to consume, but dare not get in the race
  We don't teach our children to race for resources
    We teach them to stay in their place
The dreams and desires of the masses never get fulfilled
  Because the system is only designed to steal and kill
The system design is not just predator and prey
  It is more like murder and stay
That was the foundation for the American dream
  And structural changes have yet to be seen
We still have the same issue today
  There is profit in the Middle East...so, murder and stay
They control the desires of the elite or rebels
  For access to resources
    Insidious aggression driven by deadly mental forces
If they really desired compassion and empathy
  The money wouldn't be spent on opera and symphony
As they have us trapped in the world's most violent empire
  That keeps an iron ceiling on our desires
Thoughts of freedom are changed to a different definition
  And the greedy elite stay focused on the same mission
If your thinking is externally controlled
  Then you probably don't recognize the scheme
The strategy in the U.S. is designed to control your waking life
  And your dreams
To dominate the globe

By dominating people's minds, desires, and needs
 By planting seeds of deception, acquiescence, and greed
The take away is the following lesson:
 We have to guard our thoughts and desires
  From externally imposed inception

We have not developed useful framework to help us understand that we are not on the survival track. A visual perspective may give us another way of looking at our situation. We have prepared a diagram that clarifies our political relationship with the foreign invader and hopefully inspires us to work towards freedom, which we continue to define as self-control. Politically, this is manifest as an independent black American nation. Only a mental commitment to becoming a healthy people can lead to becoming a healthy people. We refer to the concept of group survival which has been off limits for black Americans since the 1960s. Group survival is all inclusive. We use an acronym to help us awaken to the reality that group survival is necessary for us to have a future. Our current bondage is Agricultural, Spiritual, Legal, Educational, Economic, Political. We are still ASLEEP. The solution is sovereignty is each of these areas. Food sovereignty is the first one. We do not realize the need to control our food supply because we do not understand that there is a "WE." Since inception has convinced us that we are individuals, it is not well understood that we are also a group. We fail ourselves because we are only able to recognize a small portion of who we are.

Spiritually speaking, the solution is to reconnect with our roots of Animism. This undergirded our view of the world before we were invaded, enslaved and left with only the invader's religion. So, spiritual sovereignty is also historical. The legal portion is part of our defense. It gives us a concise, written description of our sovereignty so that we can defend it internationally. All of this has to be taught which is why our educational experience is extremely important. The economic piece will only be useful to the degree that it becomes divorced from greed. Africa is dominated by bribes from foreign invaders and so is black America. We have to be taught how to detach ourselves from materialism. This is absolutely required for sustainability and, therefore, required for survival.

Last but not least, we have to deal with politics. If we can see beyond the sophistry of political propaganda, then we will notice the elephant in the room is the way the "political left" is defined. We mentioned that the virus tends to mutate any time the body makes an attempt to get rid of it. In like manner, the political left has changed since the Civil Rights Movement. The other part of the struggle was the nationalist movement. This has been washed from our minds, which effectively removes the political left. The trick is that he political center is now defined as the left by pundits from all media sources. This is the only version of reality that most of us are exposed to. The following diagram is intended to help us recalibrate our sense of balance. It is intended to help us see past the political tricks that keep us bound to the same slavers from centuries ago.

The diagram is somewhat self-explanatory, but we should unpack the abbreviations of the freedom organizations that grace the political left. BCN stands for Black Christian Nationalism from the Shrine of the Black Madonna. NOI is the Nation of Islam that trained Malcolm X. RNA is the Republic of New Africa which was also a nationalist organization. Finally, the Garveyites were the followers of Marcus Garvey. He was a nationalist, but with a "back to Africa" approach. This table offers a map of the political left and political right to illustrate how this ideology is played out in the real political world. If we consider how concessions are made, then we will notice that we would have to start at the far left of the

Political Left	Off Limits 12.5% Slave	25% Slave	40% Slave	Presented Left 50% Slave	62.5% Slave	Presented Center 75% Slave	87.5% Slave	Political Right
Free			Unbossed and Unbought	M.L.K. Jr. Panthers		President Obama Nat. Act. Network Rainbow Push	Republican Party	Slave
BCN, NOI RNA Garveyites								
Self-sufficient Fully human			3/5 Freedom 3/5 Human	Illusion of equality				Political impotence
Human Rights				Civil Rights	New Civil Rights	Presented equality		No rights Subhuman
Liberation				Integration Amelioration		Mass Incarceration		Subordination Full Domination
Never Again				Autonomous but vulnerable				Fully vulnerable
Participatory Economics			Powernomics	Equitable concessions				Crony Capitalism
Create money				Living Wage		Wage slavery		No money
Sovereign land				Own property				Landless
Education			Awareness	Miseducation		Misinformation		No schooling
Food sovereignty				Own grocery stores		Grocery stores		
Justice				Fairness		New Jim Crow		
Ancestral spirituality				Slave religion				Slave religion
Unified				Organized				Scattered

we are here X

table in order to get to the middle of the table after concessions are made.

In other words, we would have to fight for nationalism just to get equality. Even though equality is the center, it is presented to us as the left. This is a nifty trick to keep us from even thinking about anything further to the left like sovereignty. So, what is presented to us as the center is actually far to the right, about halfway between absolute domination and equality. Obviously, M.L.K. Jr. fought for equality and he was killed for it. The Black Panther Party for Self Defense also fought for equality and they were destroyed as well. As a result, the new Civil Rights movement sets up further to the right.

From the table, you will notice that even if equality is achieved, we still remain 50% slaves. One reason is because the foreign invader still holds the power to allow us rights or to rescind those rights. At the equality level of achievement, we are still not able to develop a 'never again' strategy. We remain vulnerable to the dominant culture deciding to roll back any civil liberties gained which is what is actually happening as we prepare to march again. Just as equality was never achieved, the new Civil Rights movement does not actually achieve its goals either. Looking back at the diagram, we see that we fluctuate between 75% and 87.5% slavery. When we consider to what degree we are still enslaved, this table puts actual numbers to the question. This level of subordination should be totally unacceptable. Mass incarceration and police killing of our youth occur frequently with impunity because we are still roughly 80% slaves. Hopefully, this will shed some light on the debate of whether or not we are still slaves. It should also resolve the question; to what degree are we enslaved?

Hosea Williams used to champion the idea that he was unbossed and unbought. The diagram shows that he made it all the way to 3/5 human. Notice also that you are still 40% slave. You still pay taxes to the so-called white power structure. This means that you still support genocide and oppression. You may also be picked up and de-humanized at any time just because you are black. Owning your own business with black clientele will only get you to the 3/5 level of humanity. You will still not be able to express your full humanity because we are still locked into the larger context of genocidal European culture. In fact, as we have learned from many African experiences, having a politically independent nation will still not enable us to express our full humanity. If international bankers are still pulling the purse strings, then we are still in trouble. Even if we control our own finances, we are still not yet free because we will continue to exploit the Earth and our people for profit. It is only when we have totally redesigned our political economy from the bottom up that we begin on the path to liberation. One of the things to take away from this diagram is to be clear that the fight for equality is futile. We should be fighting for freedom. With this idea in mind, we will share a poem.

Equality

We remain locked into the mental framework of a madman
   Who is destroying the planet as fast as he can
Playing on our minds with scientific psychology
   Trying to convince us that we're moving toward equality
But, equality is not sharing with a thief
   In some asinine, twisted system of belief
Equality cannot be achieved until the thief goes home
   Not only that
      It requires that he leaves us and our resources alone
Equality is not accessible just because we can get a better job
   At the end of the day, we have still been robbed
Equality has not occurred when you become an entrepreneur
   While we remain in a capitalist system

That pulls morals from the sewer
If you think equality through ownership
  Will make for peace and quiet
    You have obviously forgotten about the many race riots
If you make it, the invader is coming to take it
  We know equality is off the table
  So we defensively try to fake it
We talk about utopian concepts like a level playing field
  Which is a mirage of equality
    Because these delusions are not real
Equality is a well-crafted illusion
  Just like integration as cultural fusion
As we voted for Obama and Biden
  Economic disparity continues to widen
In the 70's, we thought we had financial gains
  But today the community feels even more pain
It's a low down dirty shame
  What has been done in equality's name
Our understanding of equality has held us back
  And allowed us to remain under constant attack
Pomp and ceremony celebrate the Civil Rights battles we won
  Just empty rhetorical discussions of how far we have come
Where is the real substance to help us rise above?
  From out-of-the-box thinkers demonstrating real love?
How do we stop the exploiter's plot
  And make a genuine attempt to change our lot?
Understand this!
Equality cannot be achieved because we can vote
  It can only be achieved when we break the yoke
Between the invader and the victimized
  Keep your eyes on that prize
    Then we will rise

Equality, in the current context, depends on the political economy of the imperialist state. Politics and economics go together like wet and water. Economics is political and politics is economic. In dealing with the nature of the problem, we have to realize that the problem is not voting. The problem is the political paradigm. The problem is not jobs. The problem is the economic paradigm. Even as an independent nation, if we follow the same political economy, we will still self-destruct. In terms of solutions, we think 'voluntary simplicity' is an excellent place to start thinking about things differently as an individual and collective. One way to approach this is to minimize what we can individually be happy with rather than maximizing what we can afford. Then use the difference toward group survival. It is one of the strongest forms of resistance because it reduces our dependency on money. This works toward eliminating debt driven slavery. *A School Ma'am Looks at Money* by Anne Riley Hale is a good title in terms of how to equitably structure a money system. This holds true whether we are trying to change the current system or build our own. She recommends eliminating a debt driven system.

Another very important title is *Economic Justice and Democracy* by Robin Hahnel. He offers viable solutions to the shackles of a crony capitalist Republic. Hahnel's book primarily covers the topic of Participatory Economics (Parecon for short). More information can be readily found on the internet. There are also videos online by his research partner, Michael Albert regarding the development of Parecon. Their contribution to economic change is similar to an Indigenous American approach which can also solve the problem of sustainability. *The Power of Community* documentary film about Cuba's response to peak oil is also a powerful solution. There are countless resources and creative strategies that will allow us to become free. We just have to determine that we will define freedom in a way that will allow us to express our full humanity. We have to want to be free. We may not understand the consequences of not fighting for freedom. Suffice it to say that our survivability depends to a great extent on our ability to achieve independent decision making as opposed to following mainstream propaganda while thinking that we are making individual choices.

In the final analysis, we are suggesting that we have no logical choice except to fight for sovereignty if we intend for our children to survive. Even if all we want is equality, there is no chance of actually achieving equality in the political center unless we set up on the far left of political independence. Fighting for freedom puts us in a position to possibly win independence or to possibly achieve equality. It is almost like a win-win scenario. Fighting for equality puts us in a position to possibly achieve equality, but after concessions are made, it is more likely to leave us far to the right wherein the New Jim Crow is maintained which is presented as the political center. The only logical solution to the Black American problem of perpetual slavery is to define freedom as self-control individually and collectively. As a collective, this means that we will have to fight for sovereignty which begins with autonomous thinking manifest in autonomous communities.

An example includes the Tulsa, Oklahoma black community which was economically independent, but not self-governed. This crack in the armor allowed the Tulsa race riots to wipe out the black wealth. It was an act of war this still persists to this day. Because they had no protection, they were invaded, terrorized, and returned to dependency on the state. Therefore, an essential component of any freedom struggle must include a means of defense. Unity provides the greatest defense, but it has to be preceded by awareness and preparation. Commitments to unity are indispensable when working against a divide and conquer strategy. Voluntary simplicity will allow for a cooperative struggle and bring us to full humanity. On the contrary, continuing to buy trinkets from the dominant culture will give them more power to perpetuate our inhumanity. Is anyone else tired of injustice, tired of inequality, tired of subordination? Let's create a game called, "Who wants to be fully human?" We cannot become fully human while someone else is calling the shots, deciding which rights we can have and which we cannot. Since we are flowing into a poetic vibe again, let's move into our next poem.

Nation Time!

When we are intimidated at the voting stations
   When we are invaded with re-zoning and gentrification
When the power of our vote becomes diluted
   And the system that our vote perpetuates is polluted
When we are lied to about the vote count
   And we are left with no receipt to hold them to account
When cheating becomes the rule
   And our voting becomes a less useful tool
What time is it?
   Nation time!
When movies, television and radio prostitute our future needs
   Which is the women who bear and raise our seeds
As our children learn images that perpetuate their demise
   And the media continues to defame the character of our wise
We seem to have no control over what we see
   And our children learn
     To become the best white people they can be
We know what time it is
What time is it?
   Nation time!
Our tax dollars are spent against us and on neo-colonial wars
   While our children are left without school materials
     And nothing meaningful to study for
As the miseducation of the Negro persists

Curriculum designed to reduce black intelligence seldom exists
Educated blacks cannot lead the masses into liberation
   If they themselves have been products of miseducation
The uneducated and the miseducated
   Are like the blind leading the blind
      While the masses of our people get further and further behind
We have to control the curriculum
   In our predominantly black schools
      We have to take the initiative to make our own rules
You already know what time it is
What time is it?
   Nation time!
As the cost of health care spirals out of control
   So that we cannot care for the health of our young and our old
As a generation of obese children are more likely to die young
   We must hold ourselves accountable for what is being done
As environmental racism continues to plague us with cancers
   We cannot be blind and deaf to the sovereign answer
We are moved from ghetto to ghetto
   At the whim of the dominant culture
All made legal by the invader
   Who empowers real estate vultures
When we have finally had enough, we know what time it is
What time is it?
   Nation time!
It is time that we fly our own flag
   It is time that we make our own rules and protect what we have
We must control the images our children see
   And the curriculum they are taught
We must teach them that there is no lasting happiness in the
   Trinkets that are bought
The rites of passage for the young males
   Has become the slavery of the jail cells

So, we must control the fate of our young men
   We must write the rules so that we can win
We must control our food and water supplies
   So that we can develop a strategy to say "Never Again"
As time ticks away on our genocidal path
   We know what we must do so that our seed will last
We must Declare our Independence this time
What time is it?
Nation time!

    I am sure it has become obvious what we are trying to convey in this section. The problems with scripted resistance, diluted resistance, and co-opted resistance are all solved by becoming independent of the oppressor's rule mentally, economically, and politically. Our survival as a people fully depends on us becoming a sovereign people, not scattered sovereign individuals clinging to some obscure Moorish legality or generic African identity. This does not give us any ability whatsoever to defend ourselves. Even if we have sovereignty, wealth, institutions, etc., we still have to defend it as we have seen in the example of Libya, Iraq, etc. I have offered some poetic ways of defining freedom in this section. So that we are clear and all on the same sheet of music, so to speak, let us see how Black's Law Dictionary defines the term.

Black's Law Dictionary: <u>What is FREEDOM? definition of FREEDOM</u>
The state of being free; liberty; <u>self-determination</u>; absence of restraint; the opposite of slavery. The power of acting, in the character of a moral <u>personality,</u> according to the dictates of the will, without other check, hindrance, or <u>prohibition</u> than such as may be imposed by just and necessary laws and the duties of social life. The prevalence, in the government and <u>constitution</u> of a

country, of such a system of laws and institutions as secure civil liberty to the individual citizen.

To further reduce confusion, we will include the legal definition of self-determination.

Law Dictionary: What is SELF-DETERMINATION? definition of SELF-DETERMINATION (Black's Law Dictionary)

The fundamental right of every person to freely decide on their own political status and to pursue their own choice of economic, cultural and social development. It is embodied in the US Declaration of Independence in 1776.

These two definitions should provide some basis for unity, since it is painfully obvious, by definition, that we are still not free in 2018. It goes without saying that freedom requires unity. Neither have we achieved self-determination, with self being defined as the body of black Americans. It should be further noted that we will never be allowed to pursue this course as long as we are ruled by the world's most vicious invader who is hell bent on global domination. We offer a poem that reiterates the importance of sovereignty. It uses the four healing processes of the immune system in the solution. These were covered in more detail in our first volume, *Elusive Quest for Freedom*. We will not reprint it here. We think you will get the gist of the process from the following poem.

Sovereignty

No sovereign land, no peace
No forty acres and a mule
No sovereign economy, no peace
No money changers covering our eyes with wool
No transparency, no peace
No miseducation at school
No sovereign government, no peace

No exceptions to self-rule
No sovereign defense, no peace
No fighting for the oppressor like fools

No ancestral spirit, no survival
No imposed religious views
No food sovereignty, no survival
No starvation when we refuse
No clothing production, no survival
No sagging to keep us confused
No home building, no survival
No thirty-year debt to make us lose

No sovereignty, no freedom
  All is not lost if we can beat 'em
We only need unity to defend
  The virus must be destroyed from within
We have to recognize the enemy
  That has penetrated our hearts
And recognize when we got off to a self-destructive start
We stopped listening to our elders
  About the heroes in our past
Instead our heroes are chosen for us
  And the media makes them last

We first have to recognize the virus
  That has penetrated our culture
And has been feeding off of our innards
  Like an impatient, insane vulture
Once we have recognized the foreign destroyer
  We must neutralize its effect
By taking over our education
  And deciding what comes next

We could take full control of our communities
  If we just had the affluent and poor blacks in unity
We have to neutralize the poison by finding the antidote
  Because, the sea of equality requires a sovereign boat
The images that bombard our minds
  Are a large part of the poison that destroys our kind
If we as a people want true wealth
  Then we have to start thinking is terms of health
Once we have recognized and neutralized
  Then we have to expel the poison quickly
Otherwise we will remain the same:
  Lame, confused, and sickly
The poison is the foreign culture that must be expelled
  In the same way the human body purifies its cells
In order for Black America to expel the foreign view
  We have to be willing to start anew
To teach our young people about our pre-invasion ways
  Ensuring that we can prolong our days
We have to expel all of the foreign culture
  Because it poisons our families
    Remind our children of how to live freely and happily
Now that the virus is recognized, neutralized and expelled
  We still must remember the foreign invasion
  In order to remain well
This means remember the struggle and the fight
  To overcome a genocidal plight
Just like a virus killing you and then itself
  On an insane quest for wealth
We have to remember our own view of wealth and success
  If we want to come out of this divisive mess
We have to remember the stories
  From the vantage point of the victim
    We cannot just ask, we have to make the children listen

Remember our religious and economic system
  We can see the foreign destruction
   But we must have the courage to resist them
Recognize, neutralize, expel and remember the fight
   These things will keep us from spiraling into a genocidal night

After the piece from 2013was written for the 50th anniversary of the March on Washington, we found it necessary to include two other forms of inadequate struggle. These are misguided resistance and misdirected resistance. Taken together with scripted, diluted, and co-opted resistance, it becomes clear that very little of our freedom struggle actually contributes to our sustainable survival as a people. The masses of our people are led or misled toward fitting into the lower classes of our society with meager wage paying jobs. When Malcolm X mentioned that he wanted to be a lawyer, his teacher told him to consider something more realistic. Although we have more black lawyers today, we have an even greater number of poor blacks left without opportunity. We are misguided from the beginning of our formative years typically spent in the status quo training of our neighborhood schools. We are further misguided by the externally controlled music that our young people are invaded with on the radio.

Adults complain about how young men dress with their pants sagging below the buttocks. Dr. Welsing, one of our most notable psychiatrists, taught that this is a sign of giving up and letting the system screw you. Supposedly, it comes from the prison yard along with other prison culture that is popularized by music and videos. Giving up on the rules of society often leads to prison; but giving up on the rules of a violent and dominating society is a form or resistance. Viewed from this perspective, sagging pants is a form or resistance. Quitting the white supremacy taught at school is a form of resistance. Quoting hip hop songs that relate to our conditions is a form of resistance. Playing the music obnoxiously loud is a form of resistance. Stealing to regain some of our stolen wealth is a form of resistance. Even early procreation is a form of resistance if you understand why creatures whose lives are threatened tend to multiply faster. Misguided resistance is that which starts from the beginning. Our children are misguided from the day the start pre-K. The same is true for private school. These children are just misguided in a different way. Higher class blacks cannot escape the strategic unity necessary for the survival of the group. Higher class blacks are also misguided as demonstrated by the development of their class consciousness and self-hate for poor blacks.

Misdirected resistance comes along later in life. For example, often college students find their blackness later in life and join or create organizations for social justice. Taking their cue from previous movements, they continue to try to mold an unjust system into a just one. As was related in one of our poems, they continue the misdirected effort of trying to make chicken soup out of chicken poop. Think about what we do with the degrees we earn in academia. We may graduate in Engineering, but we are directed to use that skill to earn higher wages in this oppressive system, typically working for Europeans or Jews. We assume that making more money will enable us to do more for the poor. We are not directed to use our Engineering skills toward independent nation building as John Henrik Clarke proposed. For example, solar engineering would give the entire Global South an advantage. It would also enable us to come off the grid and be less controlled by the invaders of the Global South. Often when we start thinking about resistance, our resistance is misdirected.

We are encouraged to become entrepreneurs, but within the confines of a crony capitalist system. We think owning our own business is a form of resistance. At first glance, this appears to be the case, but business as usual does not change the status quo. The same crony capitalist direction is misdirection and there are countless African countries that have fallen for this trick if you need empirical evidence to drive this point home. The wealthy black people at the top take care of their cronies and the masses remain poor. The same system the European invaders had in place remains intact except that the people at the top are now corruptible, greedy black people instead of Europeans. Anyone who has studied this problem knows that it is essentially bribery that maintains the economic rape of Africans and their resources. The money that comes into the hands of the rich black elite is conditional. It is based on austerity, based on not helping the poor. While this problem may be subtler and more internalized, the same is true in the U.S.

We actually think capitalist-minded entrepreneurship is a form of resistance. Concerned people speak out with great volume and conviction about the need for more black businesses. We fail to realize that this does not necessarily give us more control. Yet again, our strong resistant energy is being misdirected. We are still led toward individual success as opposed to group survival. We do not think about the direction of worker-owned businesses, which is taking root globally. We do not think more broadly about owning and controlling our own resources, capital, production, and consumption. Entrepreneurship in and of itself is not liberating. When we connect it to the group-self, then we can think more clearly about distribution, about how we relate to each other economically, and about how we want to trade with each other and sell to others outside of the group.

Recall the goal of freedom is self-control, not capitalist businesses that continue to exploit the most vulnerable people in society. Since we cannot make chicken soup out of chicken poop, we will need different ingredients. Open source solar engineering is one such ingredient. Worker-owned businesses are one such ingredient. Group based dynamics rather than individually based greed will help to overcome the divide and conquer invasion. In other words, sharing rather than selfishness will lead us in the right direction. We should probably do more research into how Native Americans handle the wealth generated from casinos. We may learn something about communal involvement and distribution.

A business model example comes to mind as it relates to the recent loss of Dr. Sebi. He claimed to be able to cure AIDS, diabetes, cancer, lupus, etc. Let's assume that he could do this. Since this ability is rare and scarce, the capitalist model of distribution would make the products expensive which puts them out of reach of poor black masses who suffer from more illness than others due to increased stress and low availability of healthy food options. The capitalist model would also require the patients to come to the owner of knowledge which ensures that relatively few people without substantial income or means will get healed.

Meanwhile, dialysis centers are springing up in black neighborhoods like fast food restaurants. A more transparent and useful model would be to teach as many people as possible the techniques of this healing so that it can be taken directly to the people or at least be made more widely available. Of course, money can be made in the teaching the healing arts. Even if the inputs to production are expensive, the products could be made more affordable by soliciting the help of wealthy donors. Hospitals, especially children's hospitals, get millions of dollars in donations every year. This enables them to help people in need who do not have means of payment. Cancer research gets millions of dollars in donations every year. We could make a conscious decision to contribute to Dr. Sebi type cures instead. Then the benefits could accrue to the masses.

Just as the Black Panther Party for Self Defense established health services for poor people, Dr. Sebi's services could be made more available if there is anyone left who knows how to affect health in the way that he did. Before the Black Panthers, there were the Friendly Societies who provided health services for poor people. Please note that one of the important aspects of liberation is to become independent of European and Jewish health care domination. Cuba also has a good model of providing health care services, although it is not likely based on the mucusless diet and healing of Dr. Sebi and Arnold Ehret. This is just one example of the kind of ingredients we will need to transition to greater forms of self-control. We are currently losing large numbers of people who are victims of the biological warfare waged against us. It is not as overt as the human Ebola virus that made its way from the CDC patent in Atlanta to show up in Liberia; but many of our health problems are a consequence of biological warfare nonetheless. The healer is an important strategic player on the back row of the new chess pieces we introduced in our first book. That may be covered again later in this book. We do suggest here that even our resistance in alternative medicine is misdirected. We just want to create a healthy, happy place that we can call home.

Black home

All I want to do is to get black home
  It seems like I am in this struggle all alone
We have traded freedom for civil rights
  Individual wealth is where we aim our sights
Assuming that everything will be alright
  As the democratic process ends our plight
But democracy stole our freedom in the first place
  Democracy enslaved us as a subhuman race
Democracy is in the image of Emmit Till's face
  I cannot understand why we don't want our own space

I just want to get black home
  A place where our true skills can be honed

But we have traded independence for integration
   Given up hope for a Black American nation
Settling for the air-conditioned, corporate plantation
   While our youth are fed genocide from T.V. stations
All wishing for millions before they are thirty
   Like Mike with the clutch shot or Tiger with the birdie
It doesn't even matter if the process is dirty
   Buying studio time for empty rhymes that are wordy

I am longing for, living for a chance to get black home
   A place where justice for blacks is shown
Where is the nationalist agenda from the Nation of Islam?
   As America continues to steal from the people of Sadam
Are we afraid of freedom
   Because it would be us that they bomb?
Do we know of powerful struggles
   Like those of the Vietcong?
What is the nationalist agenda of the
  Shrine of the Black Madonna church?
   I am sure they can see our people endure so much hurt
As our women are prostituted and reduced in self-worth
   The majority keeps a watchful eye on our minority births

All I want to do is to get black home
  A place free of oppression where I can rest my bones
Our time is running out like a candle wick
  As games are played with our lives through politricks
Movements for independence give Washington a fit
  And Cointelpro destroys our ideas of freedom bit by bit
The reality of the situation is that we have been played
  As our minority status is shared with gays
And other groups of people who were never enslaved
 Our unique experience requires that we

Stand up and be brave
We have a human right to self-determination
To get black home

Chapter 3   Human Rights

Humanity

It's hard enough being human
  Consider being terrorized for hundreds of years
    Constantly filled with fear when the invader appears
Being humiliated and dehumanized by the harbingers of death
  Because monsters are hunting you down to steal your last breath
Human life has enough of its own natural troubles
  With normal conflicts we have to juggle
As we slave in the fields
  We have to send our children to school for slave teaching
    Just so we can keep breathing
Even at home the propaganda machine
  Invades their lives and dreams
To keep them from understanding
  What becoming fully human really means
We learn to think in the way we are programmed
  By social engineers
    The same ones who instill the fear
Architects of the mind
  Like stone masons that reach far back in time
    But these are masons of a different kind
No longer working with stone, like terracotta soldiers
  But with school days and air waves as our children get older
Cell phones creating mind clones as we irresistibly tune in
  Air shifters, mind benders clandestinely setting the new trend
While we are deceptively receptive to the idea that we have a voice
  We are unable to see beyond the illusion of choice
It's hard enough being human
  In a world where we can't make heads or tails
    Of what is actually true

We may be strapped, but we're trapped
  And we really don't know what to do
We can't pull ourselves up by our bootstraps
   If all we have are sandals
     It's a dirty, rotten, victim-blaming scandal
The United Terrorists of America
   Want every non-white country to be slaves
Using our taxes for the military
   So the uber-wealthy can get paid
     And keep us afraid
Imagine being dehumanized since your youth
   And never learning how to discover truth
Knowing a foreign invading culture will dominate your race
   Even if you have money, you cannot escape
You can run but you can't hide
   When your people are disenfranchised
     And your whole life you have been fed white supremacist lies
We cannot express our full humanity in this context
   So, what do we do next?
You think money will solve all your issues
   You think prosperity will make their bullets miss you
Money won't save you from your blackness
   Neither will straight hair or miseducation
We will have to take a stand to defend ourselves
   As an independent nation
Otherwise,
   We can have black pride, feel good inside
     And be happy to be alive
Meanwhile,
   Reaching our unfettered human potential is still denied
By a foreign invading culture
   Feeding off of those made poor like rabid, insane vultures
The passions of people with soul

Being robbed violently of our resources and birthright
   The masses of our people remain in this plight
It is hard enough just being human
   Without being terrorized, dehumanized, and disenfranchised
To add injury to insult, violent repression keeps us destabilized
   Every door to group progress is closed
      Making it almost impossible to rise
We are left in a world of dreams
   Because we are too afraid to open our eyes
A natural consequence of constant terror
   Purposely genocidal, not an isolated policeman's error
We are dumbed down so that we cannot recognize deceptive ploys
   As we are distracted by shiny new trinkets and toys
Dr. King said, let freedom ring
   But we cannot get there
      Because we are too focused on shiny things we call bling
It is such a sad case that we created this expression
   That finances our own oppression
It is hard enough just being human
   Makes you want to trade this life in for a new one
But we cannot
   Melvin B. Tolson said we have to save ourselves from rot
It is not enough to be alive
   The man in the torture chamber is alive
We have to remove the thorny crown
   And turn our circumstances around
The only way we can win
   Is to find ourselves worthy to defend
      And then…
         We can finally become fully human

One of the poems in the previous section entitled, *Nation Time* was interestingly inspired by Jesse Jackson. I saw an old clip of Tony Brown's journal, which used to be broadcast on PBS every Sunday. On this clip from the late 1960s or early 1970s Jesse Jackson was actually leading a call and response in which he asked "What time is it" and the crowd responded with "Nation time!" We don't know if he was just being opportunistic or whether he changed his tune because our adversary threatened his life and that of his family. It is amazing that we actually get death threats or killed just for wanting to be free of European and Jewish domination. We do not threaten their lives at all. We just want to be free. Yet we still have trouble understanding that this is not a class war. Wealthy black people are not free. As Trick Daddy said, "you still a ni&&@." Or, at least, this is the way the hyper-aggressive murderer, who denies our freedom, thinks about us. It is all about the race for resources. The "N" word is, of course, a designation and identity of inferiority created to benefit the invader. Allow us to bring out the thoughts of two scholars on this point.

Dr. Frances Cress-Welsing combined two familiar terms in her discussion of racism white supremacy. We should recognize that these two terms operate together like water and wet. Just as water is wet, racism is white supremacy. Even when black people think highly of themselves and consider Europeans to be an inferior group, black supremacists do not have the industrial military foundation to be racist anywhere in the world. In other words, blacks have no systems in place, military or otherwise, to force their views on others or to join in the race for resources. Unfortunately, we work for the military industrial complex in the United States; but we are conditioned from years of torture and terrorism to be afraid of using our knowledge and skills for our own defense. We are content with the pay we get to use our military insights to further the agenda of slavers and murderers. This effectively uses our military prowess to further oppress our own people domestically and internationally. This realization is based on being able to spread the views of the self-elevating group, not just psychologically because there is deadly physical force behind the mendacity. Racism is a deadly virus.

The meaning is made clearer in Claud Andersons's book entitled, *Powernomics* mentioned earlier. The root word of racism is, of course, race. The race involved in the etymology of the word is the race for resources. The practice of racism was, for white supremacists, to steal, kill, and destroy in the Global South. The practice of racism remains the same today as the European and Jewish virus invades Arab nations. They are racing to empower the worst in society with arms and promises in order to force regime changes that enables them to steal gold, oil, and drugs.

We learned from Joseph Carswell that this is the GOD in which they trust, which is an acronym for Gold, Oil, and Drugs. Or, we could say Gold, Oil, and Diamonds. This is the reality on the ground regardless of what we think of Christian and Jewish belief systems. We suggest that there was not significant cultivation of poppy before the U.S. invasion of Afghanistan, for example. Many sources refer to a drastic increase since then, which curiously correlates with a subsequent heroin epidemic in the U.S. It does not matter if we disbelieve internet sources about U.S. induced drug trafficking from Afghanistan because we know beyond the shadow of a doubt that this has been done for hundreds of years. A documentary entitled, *The Panama Deception* revealed the same problem with cocaine when Panama was invaded by the United States. And the infamous Opium Wars of China will never be forgotten. We express the race war in poetic form.

Race Is a Competition

To understand our situation
  We should realize that the roots of racism is a race
    And to our detriment, it is picking up the pace
Even though we did not ask to play

We are forced into this competition
This is the reality we live in
   Not my personal opinion of a racial definition
They are racing to steal and control GOD
   Which is an acronym for Gold, Oil, and Drugs
     So you see, Europeans and Jews are the real thugs
I am not talking about lightweight stuff like Cheech and Chong
   This is about robbing entire nations
     Like the Opium Wars in Hong Kong
It ain't really hurting nobody to hit the bong
   But all this global murder is dead wrong
And the perpetrators are still working through their hate list
   Using propaganda to make another group look like the terrorists
When we know it is mainly Uncle Sam and the Jewish clan
   Fanning the flame that does not need to be fanned
Racing to hell to be eternally damned
   Acting like the Devil and we call him, "the Man"
Racing to steal resources like life is a game
   Torturing and terrorizing, causing immeasurable pain
There is something wrong with the creature's brain
   Leaving his hands filthy and blood stained
It is as if someone has removed his frontal lobe
   As he races to dominate the whole globe
While trying to convince the world that the problem is Islam
   This is just another one of his racial cons
White people are the ones using the murderous forces
   In a race to steal other people's resources
Racing to destroy anyone who resists their domination
   What good are international laws
     With the U.S and Israel's flagrant violations?
Black Americans are not in a race
   Because we are not competing for anything
     We are just trying to keep from dying by avoiding death's sting

It should be obvious that we are not in a race
  In fact, we are victims of the inhumane race
    With our minds erased and bodies displaced
Which involves conditions that are not even fit for rats
  We should not acquiesce and become content with that
The race is so aggressively competitive
  That we are finding it hard to keep pace
    What is being done to us is an embarrassing disgrace
Because the aggressor continues to steal or destroy
  All the resources that we need
Deluding his group into thinking it is for their survival
  But it's just unmitigated greed
So, if we are not a race of people, who are we?
  We are 40 million beautiful black people
    Who just want to be free

The context we notice is that racism requires a hyper-aggressive willingness to kill mercilessly and indiscriminately to satisfy an insatiable greed that can only be perpetuated by those most committed to the arms race. We are back to the root word of racism. The arms race is racism white supremacy. It is unchecked aggression. The arms race has absolutely nothing to do with defense or safety. The opposite is the reality we live with as our resources are drained by incessant wars. It is offensive, not defensive and makes us less safe. Speaking of opposites, black people are not at all involved in the arms race. Black people do not have nuclear weapons. Black people do not control any military or educational system that would enable us to be racist. Let it be clear as Anderson pointed out that racism is a race. Let it be clear as Welsing pointed out, that racism is white supremacy (i.e. the race of white people toward global domination).

After reading Neely Fuller, Elizabeth Martinez and others, it occurs to me that racism (white supremacy) is a poor choice of words for non-white people to use as a description of this problem. It is similar to and heavily influenced by Great Britain. Prior to the establishment of the U.S., England was the number one terrorist murderer on the planet. Why should we call her great? There is nothing great about stealing, killing, and destroying. According to the Bible that England believes in, this behavior is Satanic. It is well documented in John 10:10.

Perhaps we should call her Satanic Britain rather than Great Britain, which is still coded in the currency as the Great Britain Pound (GBP). Given that the U.S. is responsible for even more genocidal terrorism than England, perhaps we should interpret the initials (U.S.) as Unparalleled Satanism or (U.S.A.) as Unparalleled Satanic Administration. This is the reality that we live with in the Global South. The demon seed of England is a far cry from white supremacy. The language we are using is not only intended to be compensatory, but also an accurate description of our reality as a group. We know that white supremacy is an illusion. But, when we refer to it by that name we affirm its existence. Like a mirage, an illusion does not exist in reality. Unfortunately, the poisonous deception runs so deep that we continue to use it without critique. There is no such thing as white supremacy because white people are not superior.

The deadly double-edged sword that controls our existence and subsistence is composed of violence and deception. These are the only two areas in which the global invading group is superior. Again, the same is true for a virus. The harbingers of death have a superior willingness to murder which has enabled them to develop extreme methods of psychological control. The invaders like to claim technological superiority. This is also deceptive. Most of their technological foundation is based on the stolen intellectual wealth of people from the Global South. For example, the explosives used in their murderous exploits were first developed by the Chinese who used them for celebrations. The devilish terrorists found a way to use these explosives for long distance murder. Technological superiority is actually reduced to a superior willingness to kill. We know this to be true experientially because we live with the reality of their murderous deeds every day, albeit to a lesser degree than the victims in the Middle East.

This brings us to another problem with the term white supremacy. Jews get to hide behind Semitic ethnicity. We know they are an integral part of violent global domination by their hyper-aggressive genocidal policies, not to mention the extreme defense budget charged to the U.S. taxpayer. Angela Davis has mentioned that Israel is the only country in the 21st century sill colonizing another nation. Even with every European nation voting against their aggression, Israel and the U.S. stick out, like horns on a demon, as the most Satanic of all Nations. I have seen votes as skewed as 178 to 2. The ultra-demonic nature of these two countries is unmasked.

The bankers and the military cooperate in an unprecedented violent scheme of global domination. Incidentally, this behavior is licensed by or encouraged by the first chapter of Hebrew scripture which documents the myth of Jewish Supremacy. Domination has been the goal for thousands of years. This problem did not originate with the recent ethnic amalgamation of the white race. Since white people are not superior and Jews have always been involved, we cannot correctly refer to this problem as white supremacy. The problem is European and Jewish violent and deceptive domination. Since the deception depends on the violence, the illusion of white supremacy is actually a viral infection of hyper-aggressive European and Jewish violence. The race is the systematic killing of people for their land, resources, labor, and intellectual capital.

What we think is superior intellect is often stolen from the people they invade. The culture of the invaders is also not superior. Obviously, it is a culture of destruction. It destroys not only people, but all living things are affected. Some are driven into extinction. The capitalist economic paradigm is not superior either. Neither is it sustainable since it is based on slavery and perpetual growth which cannot be achieved. It depends on over-exploitation of all the Earth's resources. Sadly, agricultural and pharmaceutical industries seem to work together to deprive us of the nourishment we need so we will be forced into dependency on pill-pushing doctors. This forces us into dependency on the medical, pharmaceutical, and insurance industries. Hypertension, diabetes, and other illnesses are directly related to the food choices we are given. Then the problems are blamed on the consumer's choice. Biological warfare is part of the violence while psychological warfare spins the truth. The mental invasion obfuscates truth as we are coerced into embracing delusions.

Governments are supposed to care for the people and the Earth because they are made up of the people who rely on the Earth. Instead, they choose domination over caring by enacting anti-life policies that spread poverty and suffering. This is not superior. In the final analysis, only a superior willingness to kill remains. Since stealing, killing, and destroying do not make a group superior, there is no such thing as white supremacy or Jewish supremacy. Rather than bringing civilization, technology, and religion, these groups have brought death and destruction to the Global South. Everyone is not deceived. We will try to refrain from referring to the genocidal system of domination as white supremacy which affirms superiority. Our liberation requires that we call it correctly by name. It can be correctly described as a genocidal system of domination perpetrated by Europeans and Jews. Confucius said, "The beginning of wisdom is to call things by their proper name."

Fuller points out that racism can only be perpetrated by Europeans because they are the only ones who have a stranglehold on everyone else. Anderson wrote that racism can only mean

Europeans because they were the only ones in the race when this problem was conceived, and they have violently kept anyone else from entering that race for resources and domination. While other nations have practiced ruthless imperialism, it is clear that the merciless aggression from Western Europe is unprecedented. Three other things should be mentioned about the illusion of white supremacy and Jewish supremacy. First, a few more words about the origin are necessary. Second, the reasoning or logic for the practice of violent domination is important. Third, the question of genes or memes has to be dealt with in order to develop a proper solution.

      We have already discussed the Hebrew scriptural origin in which God is said to have given dominion to Hebrews which is an identity taken over by modern day Europeanized Jews. The scribes additionally wrote about God's blessing in the murder of their neighbors who had different spiritual views. We all know this is the model Europeans used in their invasions of the Global South. Christianity was spread with the worst forms of violence and terrorism in the history of the world. As it was with the Hebrews, divine providence was their justification. So, in one sense, the origin of European and Jewish genocidal domination is a brain child of Hebrew leadership which is well documented in the Torah and Bible.

      Another aspect of this problem has roots in classism. The superiority complex is not only a Hebrew religious construct, but also a European societal construct. The ruling elite stood in stark contrast to the inferior masses. The superior/inferior relationship was already well developed long before it was imposed on the Global South. This problem seems to have first begun with ethnic supremacy (within a single nation). People of the ruling elite were of particular blood lines. Classism is not only a social construct; it also has roots in genetic domination. Both genes and memes come into play.

Beyond ethnic supremacy, this viral sickness of violent domination mutated into national supremacy (between nations such as England and Spain). This also marks the beginning of the arms race. European nations built up armaments to demonstrate their superiority and Jews helped to finance their wars with each other. The Bible calls them money changers. Beyond national supremacy, the problem mutated into the illusion of white supremacy which put poor whites in charge of blacks. This strategic move unified whites from various nations and divided poor whites and poor blacks who were in the same economic class. This model spread like a virus across the Global South. We would like to reiterate that a greater willingness and ability to kill does not make a group superior whether it is an ethnic group, a nation, or a subcontinent of people.

Supremacy has to do with superiority whereas domination has to do with a power relationship. The real problem is the violently forced, unjustifiable, asymmetric power relationship. Let's think about some of the reasons for establishing this inequity. It certainly has nothing to do with the pursuit of happiness. If that were the case, we would probably all be following Buddha or Animism on a non-theistic path to Enlightenment or Nirvana. Instead, aggressive groups choose a path that we will describe by a book subtitle: *The Pathological Pursuit of Profit and Power*. (Bakan 2005) Rather than go into great detail, we will just list a few other reasons why some people and groups desire domination of others: narcissism (unbridled ego), greed, insanity, jealousy/envy, imperialism, mismanagement of resources, and fear. Allow me to offer a quick note on the last two. It is not often mentioned that a primary driver of the race for resources was poor management practices at home. This necessitated the need to find resources elsewhere because of a refusal to try to live sustainably. Profit was prioritized. In addition to mismanagement, there is the fear that if we do not overtake them, they may try to overtake us.

Whether consciously or unconsciously, this is only justification for ignorance and greed.

Of course, this overlaps the discussion about deception. Fear is often manufactured for the purpose of resource theft and domination as we currently witness in the Arab world, especially in Iraq and Syria. Again, a book title is insightful here. Is the reason for this aggression *Hegemony or Survival?* (Chomsky 2003) The object of fear used to be the practice of a different religion. Killers were led to believe that people of a different religion had to be murdered as was done in the Bible with God's blessing. Then the fearmongering became attached to people from a different culture or color. Killers are made afraid of black people or so-called Indians so they are targeted for death. Then there was the fear of communism. Now it is the fear of terrorism. This fear is manufactured so that the resources of the Arab world can be stolen and the people can be dominated. This is not white supremacy. It is genocidal aggression perpetrated by so-called Whites and Semites. Arabs are not terrorizing the United States or Israel. In reality, the U.S. and Israel are terrorizing Arabs. No treatment of this topic would be complete, however, without mentioning a fear that may not be manufactured, but still works to our detriment.

According to Dr. Frances Cress-Welsing, the so-called problem of white supremacy may be motivated by a fear of genetic annihilation. If this is truly a survival instinct, then the problem may be genetic rather than social. We have demonstrated that in many aspects, the problem of violent, genocidal aggression is social (memes). But we have also shown how the problem may also be genetic (genes). Within nations, there is ethnic bloodline domination. Globally, there is subcontinent group domination (white/non-white). The question as to whether the problem stems from genes or memes has been answered as "both."

There is the genetic fear of disappearing if whites get to friendly with black people in particular. Intermixing will cause white people to cease to exist. This fear is terribly exacerbated by insatiable greed. We have to approach this problem carefully so that we do not leave out any aspects. If we leave out parts of the cancer, it will spread again. The better we understand the innerworkings of this problem, the better we will be able to devise and implement a sustainable solution. The Hebrews set out to dominate all things. Europeans signed on to this ideology of superiority in the quest for global domination. As we liberate ourselves, we will be liberating the whole planet from European and Jewish violent domination. As demonstrated in the following poem, the psychology of white supremacy is yet another falsification passed off as a legitimate and logical. Then we share a poem about the enemy.

Illusion of White Supremacy

The illusion of white supremacy seems to be on the rise
   And this comes as no surprise
Because European invaders have taken many things for granted
   Now that their domination is waning, they are in a panic
It turns out that white supremacy has really been a lie
   Just murderous thieves causing other people to die
Then written down as legal codes to live by
   And even though the sky is blue
      We know that blues don't come from the sky
Sad and despondent blues come from Northern invaders
   Who, incidentally think that they are greater
By virtue of being the best at murder
   Stopping peaceful people from advancing further
How superior is that?
   Always aggressively on the attack
There is no such thing as white supremacists
   These are Whites of Mass Destruction (WMDs)

   Without delay or interruption
The genocide has been persistent
   Inclined to follow a satanic divine, and resistant
Not open to equality or diversity
   Like a raging boar still waging wars of adversity
White supremacy is an illusion
   Supporting many other fatal delusions
     I can only draw one conclusion
The harbingers of death
   Are going to have to move to the left
     To, at least, let the Earth catch her breath
From all the poisons and abuse
   The intellect we have been taught as supreme is really obtuse
I just want to know the answer to one simple thing
   If the European Diaspora is really supreme
Why do they always have to kill?
   This is clearly the precursor to all other skills
So which part is superior…stealing, killing, or destroying?
   This twisted, iron fisted logic is more than annoying
     With gunships and drones continuously deploying
Hundreds of years of terror
   By design, not by error
The misguided logic is fatal
   From the tomb to the cradle
White supremacy is not a reality
   It is just a murderous mentality
That makes a certain people feel great
   Of course, this has been a deadly mistake
What has been taught to us as progress
   Has really been a global domination quest
We have to realize what is at stake
   Before we reach a point of no return
     We better stop the madness before it's too late

Enemies of Freedom

We have the freedom to sit in the front of the enemy's bus
  In route to the city plantation
Freedom to vote for the enemy
Freedom to run for office in the enemy's political system
Freedom to go to enemy schools
  Assuming we are too dumb or inferior to establish better schools
Freedom to join the enemy's military
Freedom to dine at the enemy's restaurant
Freedom to work for the enemy
  For less than what our families need
Freedom to sell our land to the enemy
Freedom to utilize enemy food stores
Freedom to denounce our own spirituality
  To accept the enemy's religion
Freedom to be guided into our history by the enemy
Freedom to be guided into our future by the enemy
Freedom to be a capitalist, but not otherwise
Freedom to be a citizen of an enemy nation
Freedom to live as a number
Freedom to be democratic, like the democrats who enslaved us
Freedom to be taxed by an enemy collector
Freedom to have the death and taxes and trouble
  That Marvin Gaye sang about
Freedom to speak the enemy's tongue
Freedom to play the enemy's game
Freedom to treat life as a game
Freedom to be fingerprinted and foot printed
  As soon as you come into the world
Freedom to stand in the enemy's soup line
Freedom to be exploited in athletics and entertainment

Freedom to rot in prison
Freedom to pay for degrees of education, which cannot be shared
Freedom to write enemy phonics
Get the point?

True to our Black American Liberation Language, it is befitting to include with this topic a poem about the language that we are familiar with. Language carries energy. This energy can help us or hurt us. We argue that the current language that we have learned to use is hurting us. As a negative affirmation, the usage of white supremacy is self-defeating. It also keeps us from defining the problem specifically enough to deal with it appropriately. Toward creating a mindset that leads us in the direction of solving the problem, we offer the following poem.

The Truth of Things

The language we use is important
  It can create harmony or discordance
For example
  Here is a sample
Our people should know that white supremacy is a misnomer
  We cannot seem to see it because of psychological glaucoma
White supremacy does not actually exist
  But the ideology persists
    Evidenced by the fact that we are still on the kill list
When they came to our lands, we were hospitable hosts
  After stealing, killing, and destroying
    Now they have us chasing ghosts
We cannot fight against something that is not really there
  As we try to change our imposed society
    Into something that's more fair
Many terrorist years of brain trauma and confusion

Has caused us to accept this problem we define as an illusion
Then we wonder why there is no restitution
  Or meaningful solution
We are still stuck on an inferiority/ superiority complex
  That our language has not allowed us to overcome yet
Because there are blinders and restraints on our perception
  Which keeps us down as we continue to fall prey to deception
Although white supremacy does not exist, the deception is real
  It convinces us that invaders are superior
    Since they destroy, kill, and steal
Confucius said the beginning of wisdom
  Is to call things by their right name
If we want to overcome circular progress
  And affect real change
Institutions are not built on white supremacy
  They are built on domination
Thwarting our survival needs
  To build an independent black nation
It is not white supremacy killing us every 28 hours
  It is demonic aggression
We cannot solve this problem
  With a white supremacist obsession
We certainly need mental defense
  But we need physical defense as well
We have to protect our people
  From mass incarceration and murderous hell
Superiority and inferiority are part of the classism that divides us
  Keeping us from developing relationships of trust
    Unity is a must
Emulating the oppressor is the opposite of unity
  Getting money and acting funny does not help the community
White supremacy is not the cause of this problem
  It is the external control of our minds

Deception controlling our perception
  Making solutions hard to find
It is not white supremacy. It is miseducation
  Blocking off neural pathways
    Causing poor judgement and mental frustration
It is not white supremacy. It is the radio
  Abusing us, confusing us about which is the right way to go
Our movements for improvements never seem to last
  Because the violence from the invader
    Ultimately determines our path
We end up on the road of least resistance so that we can stay alive
  Ignoring that this is not our true destiny
    This is ruthlessly contrived
The problem is not white supremacy
  It is violent, deceptive domination
We have to call the problem by its true name
  To begin to take away its power and work toward cessation

Our language cannot compensate enough for the terror we experience from the ruthless lot of murderers that hold us in bondage. If we are familiar with Emma Lazarus' poem entitled, *The New Colossus* which is inscribed on the Statue of Liberty, it would help put this problem in perspective. Bear in mind that the only thing our children learn in school is the illusion of white supremacy, even in math class. All black children should be familiar with this poem so that it can help to counterbalance the inferiority complex that is developed in our children as they imbibe and internalize a deceptive and inferior view of the world. We have written a poem around Lazarus that we will share here. It is a poem within a poem.

Colossus

President Obama said the United States
   Has the strongest military in the world
      But what does this mean?
Perhaps we can glean something from the words
   Of Dr. Martin Luther King
He said the U.S. is the greatest purveyor of violence
   In the world today...and that was in 1968
      Is it murder that makes this country great?
Meanwhile, we are programmed to support our troops
   Number one terrorist in the world, thou art loosed
The U.S. is the number one weapons dealer on the planet
   We take our violent insecurity for granted
Noam Chomsky said the number one threat to world peace
   Is the United States self-appointing itself as the global police
Journalist and hip hop artist Akala said that murder runs the globe
   It has become painfully obvious that the emperor has no clothes
We can see the naked aggression and violent orchestration
   To set up a system of unchallenged domination
We now know the U.S. to be the greatest purveyor of violence
   In the history of mankind
      When we uncover the perpetrators, what do we find?
Several layers of deception with sanitized versions of the past
   Hiding the fact that the U.S. is populated by
      And run by merciless white trash
As incendiary as this may sound, fire brings things to light
   Burning away the veil of delusions, leaving truth in plain sight
Like the migration poem by Emma Lazarus
   Available for us all to see
Engraved boldly and coldly
   On the colossal Statue of Liberty

The New Colossus

Not like the brazen giant of Greek fame,

With conquering limbs astride from land to land;

Here at our sea-washed, sunset gates shall stand

A mighty woman with a torch, whose flame

Is the imprisoned lightning, and her name

Mother of Exiles. From her beacon-hand

Glows world-wide welcome; her mild eyes command

The air-bridged harbor that twin cities frame.

"Keep ancient lands, your storied pomp!" cries she

With silent lips. "Give me your tired, your poor,

Your huddled masses yearning to breathe free,

The wretched refuse of your teeming shore.

Send these, the homeless, tempest-tost to me,

I lift my lamp beside the golden door!"

Did she say Mother of Exiles?
   We should immediately recognize that something has run afoul
Like excrement from the bowels of European lands
   Torturing and terrorizing indigenous people for their resources
That is the plan
     So, don't think that we don't understand

But we are dealing with the most violent people
  In the history of humanity
And this group actually feels as though they are superior
  It's insanity
So if I say the U.S. is populated by white trash
  Don't assume this is verbal abuse
    Emma Lazarus' poem said, "give me...the wretched refuse"
It doesn't matter what fiction you have learned to believe
  United States' greatness is based on murdering thieves
The U.S. is not run by superior minds
  Or technologically developed by a superior kind
These are the same genocidal maniacs from the distant past
  The U.S. is run by and supported by monstrous white trash
For those of you who cannot digest this truth
  Because I didn't mask it or cloak it
    Put that in your white supremacy pipe and smoke it

As Donald Trump was running for president in 2016, we saw a second spike in white supremacist groups as Obama's term was ending. With this presidential candidate they have been emboldened. He clearly has a large constituency of white supremacists following him. In September of 2016 we penned a poem after hearing his nauseating slogan. Let's see how we get from the white trash on the Statue of Liberty to perceived greatness.

Hate

Who is it that loves to hate?
  Making poverty of other people's fate
Who hates to share
  But loves to steal
Hates peace

But loves to kill
Hates diplomacy
  But loves drone strikes
    Loves to bomb the masses after midnight
Hates transparency
  But loves stealth bombs
Hates indigenous people
  But loves brutal dictators and uncle Toms
Hates egalitarian
  But loves totalitarian
Hates Fidel Castro
  But loves Augusto Pinochet
Still hunting Assata Shakur
  Even to this very day
Hates even trades
  But loves money tricks
Hates the honest poor
  But loves rich thieves who make us sick
Hates autonomous nations
  But loves central banks
Hates Arabs who won't pay interest
  But loves Jews like their sh!# don't stank
Hates peace and harmony
  But loves a tumultuous rift
    Israel's military just got a 38 billion dollar gift
Hates truth
  But loves lies
Hates journalists
  But loves spies
Hates the righteous
  But loves the wrong
Hates a square deal
  But loves a dirty con

Hates Bradley Manning and Julian Assange
Hates any peace loving nation
  But loves to murder for global domination
Hates red, black, and brown people
  But loves their land
    Hates insurgency when the people take a stand
Hates love
  But loves hate
This is the real United States
Hates to love
  But loves to hate
    Is this what makes us great?

It should be clear that the European and Jewish incursion of the Global South is, without precedent and without equal, the worst murderous atrocity in the history of the world. These harbingers of death are also allegedly, but unambiguously, responsible for the monstrous mendacity of Sep. 11, 2001. It was sloppily blamed on Muslims as a pretext for invasion of the Middle East. We should know that the real Sep. 11th was in 1973 which involved the same perpetrators and the same genocide. I mention this because most people will not be aware of Augusto Pinochet who was mentioned in the *Hate* poem above. You should also be aware of the 38 billion dollars that President Obama signed over to Israel's military. In some United Nations votes, the only two countries that vote for continued aggression are the U.S. and Israel. The votes stand against the wishes of the rest of the world to include all other European countries. If it seems very undemocratic, it is. If it seems like bullying, it is.

Unfortunately, millions of people are still being murdered and displaced today, not unlike the global invasions and terrorism from 500 years ago. It is not only morally reprehensible; it is destructive for the invader and the indigenous. They are killing everybody and everything in order to dominate. The invader becomes dependent on the land, labor and resources of indigenous people, flora, and fauna. Meanwhile, indigenous people are robbed of their means of survival and thus, must seek a job with the invader. We become assimilated into a culture that destroys not only the relationship between the two direct parties, but also destroys our relationship with the environment which we are forcing into a death spiral. We are experiencing the outcome of living under the illusion of white supremacy which includes Jewish supremacy. A greater awareness of reality is enabling us to discover the truths necessary to establish harmonious relationships.

The greediest and most violent country in the history of the world is the U.S. A. Yet, we do not make the connection between, genocide, slavery, capitalism, and so-called progress. These are obviously intertwined. The beneficiaries of the continual invasions are not incentivized to want this problem solved. It is designed to be a self-reinforcing system. So, we have to work outside of the box. We have to change the rules of engagement. We have to change the paradigm. We are going to need unity with entertainers, athletes, and actors. We are being destroyed as one people whether rich or poor. Ask Bill Cosby or Michael Jordan what happened to their murdered family members. Like it or not, we are one people. Black Americans are a group worthy of survival as an entity. We will also need international help from countries the U.S. cannot easily invade and dominate. Churches could provide scholarships for language gifted children to study abroad in places that can help us liberate ourselves and defend our people from constant murders and other human rights violations.

Of course, getting to this step means that we have to follow the pre-requisite of a self-liberating mental path. This means getting out of the box, which is to say getting out of the schools and out of the view and sound of mainstream mediums of propaganda. Our efforts are complicated by our spiritual path, our moral path. The slaving religious system of the invader limits our world view to that of perpetual slaves. It tends to reduce the solution set to status quo window dressing. We have to change the window through which we see the world. Liberation requires that we have windows that allow for unlimited light. Enlightenment means something different to black American people than it does in Eurocentric history books. Our spiritual path has to be co-liberated with our mental path in order to move into a direction of freedom.

While it is necessary to use the powerful energy of our painful African past, we must also learn to use the varying degrees of our inner diversity. We have connections with other people and lands. We are more than African and we can draw from more than African mentally, emotionally, and spiritually. We are also Asian, Latin American, European, Native American and Indian. Our inner diversity is a necessary creative key to our survival. African is only part of our identity. We have to identify with the rest of who we are in order to draw from the fullness of possibilities. Again, we have to change the window in order to allow for more light. Black American does not mean the same as African. We are not only more complicated culturally, we are also more complicated biologically. It makes it more difficult to unify, but it is imperative that we use all of who we are in our bid for survival over greed and violence.

We will come back to the topic of our identity. For now, let's deal with the violence. We have a poem written years ago that reaches back to the symbolic, poetic fight of the 1980s just prior to gangster rap which led us into the current period of empty or destructive lyrics. This poem was written with hip hop in mind and compensates for the aggression of the invader, but only symbolically. We do not wish any harm on the invader. Again, we just want to be free from his domination. Powerful language is required to awaken us from our slaving slumber. This next poem uses such provocative language.

Lynch Uncle Sam

What's really happening with the lyrics in hip-hop?
  Gangster rap or not
    My brothers and sisters are headed for prison, non-stop
Like it's a Rites of Passage to become an adult
  Spit on the mic like a satanic slavery cult
It's not all good. All is not well
  And it should be obvious that we are not thinking for ourselves
Who is the puppeteer pulling the strings?
  Out of sight and behind the scenes
    Defining what our lives mean?
Keeping us confined in our minds
  To a self-destructive grind
    As we exploit our own kind
Reduced to bragging about pimping and slinging dope
  Somebody find me a rope
But we are going past the mindless rapper to take it to the man
  It's time to lynch Uncle Sam

Check it out! I've got a real itch
  Because, you know pay back is a bitch
Burning my brothers in a wood pile
  Wasn't that his style?
Well, that injustice was real foul
  And now we're about to get buck wild
He's been controlling our minds for too long
  Got my brothers and sisters going wrong
But now, we have a new song
  And the vibe is real strong

We should have known all along
   What was really going on
While knuckleheads on the street are pimping their own
   Smoking weed every day and sipping Patron
Thinking we are coming up by putting our women down
   Shucking and jiving like minstrel faced clowns
It should be easy to see
   That it is time to find a timberland tree
In order to free the people, we need a plan
   Let's lynch Uncle Sam

My brothers and sisters sell the people out for large amounts
   Now, we have to hold them to account
Many started out in the ghetto
   But they get the money and bounce
You know they're dead wrong
   But I am here to announce
Trimming the leaves off the problems
   Is not going to solve them
We have to take it to the source
   To the puppeteer, of course
When brothers like Dead Prez get no air play
   What do you think we are going to hear on the radio every day?
It is the folks behind the scene
   Controlling the green
Not the brother's on front street
   With the bling-bling
We are being fed gangster garbage
   From the media owners
And the advertisers known as
   The corporate donors
So everybody rushes to make denigrating music
   And exploiters continue to abuse it

It's time we begin to make some real demands
　It's time to lynch Uncle Sam

Not long ago, we were seeing nooses everywhere
　We let it pass by us as if we didn't care
Nooses in the office, in construction, in schools, in trees
　Negro please!
Are we supposed to excuse these terrorist threats of hanging
　Because they hired Obama to convince us things are changing?
The game only changes names
　While things remain the same
We have heretofore been overly reticent
　It's time to give him a dose of his own medicine
The slave programming is wearing off
　So, he'd better get ready to pay the cost
Pay the piper or the sniper. It's his own choice
　Because now the real black man's going to have a voice
His devilish ways have been uncovered
　And he cannot get me to divide from my brothers
While trying to sell us stars with no light
　Knowing their ways ain't right
While keeping the useful role models out of sight
　So my people cannot rise to higher heights
Well, we are going to create a new game
　We're watching Uncle Sam hang

　　It is said that a picture is worth a thousand words. For this reason, we are including several visual aids with this poetry. While my artistic ability is comparable to the drawing of stick people, we trust that the message is still adequately conveyed. The following visual aid depicts the initial process of globalization which we have entitled, *Going Viral*. This comes about partially because Hillary Clinton had the audacity to repeat her position from the

1990s and called black people super predators. The context was a situation in which Black Lives Matter activists cornered the Clintons about Bill Clinton's policies of mass incarceration which further destroyed many black communities. In defense of her husband, Hillary unapologetically said that it was super predators [black people] that were being locked away. This echoed the sentiment of the previous generation as we were depicted as lawless madmen in the media during the crack epidemic of the late 1980s and 1990s. In the case of the most vulnerable in U.S. society, what we have is super projection. That is to say the invading group projects its faults onto the defenseless group. The following diagram shows the unadulterated reality of super predators.

Going Viral

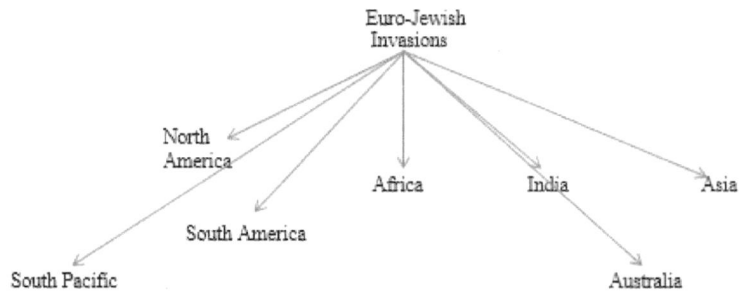

This simple sketch illustrates the ongoing invasion of the Global South. It shows hyper-aggression gone exponentially bad. It simply puts a visual representation to the reality that Europeans spread merciless violence to the far reaches of the globe. Western Europeans, without equal, are the most violent people in the human family. And we know Jews were involved, so we are including them as well. What was done in the past is still being done today. Europeans and Jews are the actual super predators, the harbingers of death that are destroying the entire planet for profit. To illustrate the exponentially worsening situation, we will denote this initial aggression with the symbol $\mathcal{E}$. More specifically in this global catastrophe, the English were the most involved. Follow the money, as it is said. The British Empire became enriched with its invasions of Africa, India, China, North America, etc. The English demonstrated that they are far more violently aggressive than Europeans in general. We will denote this aggression by $\mathcal{E}^2$. The third level is punctuated by the invasion of what is now the U.S. The invaders of the United States are even more violent and ruthless than the British, as evidenced by the Revolutionary War and the war of 1812 which was fought over who would get the spoils of genocide and slavery. We will denote this aggression by $\mathcal{E}^3$.

  We are aware that this is not the sanitized version of the story that is brainwashed into our children in U.S. schools. It is obvious that the invader is never going to tell the truth about the despicable evil involved in his invasions. Dr. Gerald Horne penned a view with greater insight in *The Counter-Revolution of 1776: Slave Resistance and the Origins of the United States of America*. It is a very detailed account of what actually happened leading up to 1776 including the motivations and the money trail. When we combine this knowledge with *The Shock Doctrine: The Rise of Disaster Capitalism* by Naomi Klein and *Hegemony or Survival: America's Quest for Global Dominance* by Noam Chomsky, it is undeniable that Europeans in the U.S. are the greatest terrorists in the history of the world and in the contemporary world. Violence at this level is unprecedented and far beyond the initial European invasions, so we have used $\mathcal{E}^3$ to symbolize European and Jewish violence to the third power. This is what we mean by levels of violence that became exponentially worse. Of course, we have a poem on this topic not surprisingly titled, Empire.

Empire

Part 1
Lest we get our perceptions twisted by mainstream propaganda
　We should recall the so-called greatness of Alexander
We must remember that empires are built on genocidal violence
　An empirical reality of which I cannot be silent
Exploitation, devastation
　These are the result of an empire's endless invasions
A genocidal war was waged in Iraq
　In order to steal the resources and dominate the region
　　The problems with this kind of devilish terrorism are legion
Red, black, and brown people know this all too well
　For hundreds of years, we have been living with his hell
But ISIS rose from the ashes like a phoenix from hell fire
　To challenge the domination of the great Satan's empire
Bringing the U.S. back to complete the genocide
　In light of historical precedent, this comes as no surprise
The white house and the Pentagon are still telling the same lies
　Like fracking they're attacking the Sunni-Shiite divide
Pursuing like a virus from the inside and outside
　To rule out any possibility of Iraqi homeland pride
President Obama said he would degrade and destroy these Iraqis
　In their own nation state
Ethnic tensions he would exacerbate
　So that he could enlist other Arabs to participate
Disillusioned rebels paid handsomely to join the malaise
　Freedom and justice are buried somewhere deep beneath the fray
This sounds eerily like Ferguson, Missouri
　Where the degraded and destroyed look like you and me
They define and denigrate in order to destabilize and defeat
　The methodology is to invade, enslave or colonize...then repeat
The freedom of the European and Jewish diaspora

Has required the violent bondage of the Global South
  A situation of abject subordination
    From which we have yet to come out
The liberty of those who are typically considered white
  Brings torture, terrorism, and despair
    To those without drones in flight
A blight in the Earth
 A plight of our diminished self-worth
   Allowing demons to reign like an evil curse
This is more than a kerfuffle
  This is mass extinction kind of trouble
That we tend to ignore as we are so easily distracted
  Until, of course, our immediate families are impacted
Being dehumanized has robbed us of empathy
  So that we don't feel the pain
    Of the terrorized Global South in Democracy's name
Still worse, we join the U.S. military
  And directly support murder indiscriminately
Rather than fighting for our own survival and justice
  So we can live self-sufficiently
Truth is polluted and convoluted in the murderous games they play
  Like the dumbest of dumb our minds are made numb
    As we're stuck with war bills to pay
Warmonger denizens tricking the citizens
  Support our troops they say
It becomes clear year after year
  That genocide is the American way

Part 2
So, how do we overcome?
  How do we reverse the damage that is being done?
Liberation from the badges and incidents of slavery
  Will require some sacrifice and bravery

Spiritually, mentally, and physically reconnecting with the land
   This is how we overcome the white-boy
     Whom we think is the man
What does spiritual liberation look like?
   To bring us out of the distracted world of darkness
     Into limitless insight
Well, it doesn't look like Christianity or Islam
   To whose empires we succumbed
     Invading us with swords, ideology, diseases, and guns
It looks more like red, black, and brown Earth
   Without the religious disguise
The study of truth
   Cuts psychological warfare and propaganda down to size
Reconnecting with the land and each other
   Will essentially make our spirituality fool proof
Which brings us to the schools that make us fools
   In the way that they teach our youth
The system is never going to teach our children
   How to become free from domination
They will only be offered the white supremacy and tokenism
   Of a status quo education
But the training of our children
   Can be controlled by community led organizations
Which should naturally and justifiably
   Lead us to develop a sovereign nation
This is a strategy by which justice can prevail
   A self-reliant way a broken and sick people can get well
The individualism of divide and conquer is tearing us apart
   We accept it, even embrace it and this is not smart
One of the most important things we can inculcate in our youth
   Is the paramount importance of reconnecting as a group
We must be relentless in our pursuit of group survival
   To overcome the hyper-aggressive violence of our rivals

We have to fight for survival together
  If we truly want things to get better
Our physical liberation is dependent on our education
  Of which both are dependent on our spiritual foundation
Our success cannot depend on our demise
  As our investment guidance belies
 We end up giving more resources to the white power structure
  Like our economic brain cells have ruptured
We have to manipulate the money
  And stop letting the money changers manipulate us
We must invest in nation building skills to overcome the ills
  And develop mutual trust
So that we can produce and distribute what we need
  While we develop spiritually
    Tto rise above individualism and greed
In an effort to find freedom and lasting happiness
  We have to think beyond the ego
Which can be done if we study hard to find truth
  And practice what we know
The interconnectedness of our group is truly divine
Things will work out fine
  Aas we stay focused and unwavering over time
As long as freedom is an uncompromising desire
 We can overcome this degrading, dangerous, delusional,
   dominating, dehumanizing, destabilizing,
    deplorable, demonic, destructive,
      Empire

We will just briefly sketch an outline of the possible reasons or motivation behind the behavior that destroys us. The following are the five fundamental reasons for European and Jewish invasion of the Global South which is manifest in genocide and slavery/colonialism:

1. Ecological ignorance—
   This involves a lack of understanding or misunderstanding regarding the connectedness of living things in an environment. It is all about respectful relationships. We have been victims of unnatural predator-prey relations that destroy the possibility of human harmony while also creating imbalances among all other living things on the planet. The European and Jewish advancement is destroying everything on the planet, not just black people. They did not listen to our ancestors whom they ignored and invaded. They burned books and destroyed knowledge so that they could seem superior. This demonstrates extreme ecological ignorance.
2. Pathological pursuit of profit and power—
   Unmitigated greed is an essential component of this. There is a book with this subtitle that we encourage you to read. If you absolutely do not have time, then we direct you to the documentary entitled *The Corporation*. It covers the same information. It will help you to understand some of the inner-workings of capitalism that are essential to the planning of our liberated future. We cannot take the same view of money as the slaver and use the same business practices. Otherwise, we will continue the same problem with new masters. This has happened in several African countries because the leaders have taken on the same economic mentality as the invader.
3. Cress Theory of Color Confrontation—
   The basic premise of her theory is that fear of genetic annihilation stimulates hyper-aggressive behavior against people of color. We don't necessarily agree with this, but it is still important to know. While it is true that the threat of genetic annihilation exists, we recall the history of extreme

violence as Europeans fought against each other even before they went abroad to steal, kill, and destroy. This was long before they began to terrorize and torment the Global South.

4. Dominion, as it is sanctioned in the first chapter of the Bible—

The practice here is to kill until unchallenged domination is made possible. This frame of mind comes from the Hebrews which is an identity taken over by present day Jews. This may not be the origin of documenting a superiority complex, but it has certainly lent itself to invading others with divine blessing. Being the favorite of God is a superiority complex. Having dominion over others is a superiority complex. Whether those others are people or animals is irrelevant since people are animals, which brings up our next point.

5. Animal labor—

Slave labor of animals is a slippery slope to slave labor of humans since humans are also animals. This part of the problem, of course, begins with extreme physical violence, but is perpetuated mostly by psychological conditioning with periodic violence not unlike Pavlov's bell. This also underscores why it is of paramount importance for us to understand liberation in a way that was developed by a culture of people who had no slave animals. The indigenous culture of North America is one such group. It is right under our nose. They had no animal slaves which also gives us context for understanding the twisted view of historians who tell us that Indigenous Americans owned black slaves. Indigenous people are still not capitalists today, so why would we believe they were slave owners 200 years ago? It is important for us to learn to live without slave labor. Europeans and Jews will have to learn to live without exploiting others. Otherwise, the ecological system will not only remain out of balance, but the problem will accelerate and hasten our demise.

In order to reverse problems of aggression, we will have to learn to think differently. We do not seem to understand the logic of liberation which could be abbreviated as (lol). Instead, we make an acronym out of laugh out loud (lol). Well, perpetual slavery is not funny, and it does not make us proud. James Brown said, "I'm black and I'm proud." That is a good first step; but I'm free and I'm proud would be even better. We cannot seem to get there because we do not teach our children about freedom. As a result, they are not using their very active energy and mental quickness to move toward freedom. We teach our children about African history and Civil Rights. Then we end up poisoning that knowledge by teaching them about individual material success within the confines of capitalism. We teach them white supremacy by teaching them that the best schools and the most desirable schools are white schools. In so doing, we teach them implicitly that European invaders are the smart people with all the answers. As a consequence, we end up operating from a mental foundation infected by an inferiority complex. So-called educated black people end up with mental health issues unable to rid themselves of the virus. Typically, we are not able to recognize the presence and influence of the virus that we have become so accustomed to making excuses for. We assume we are actually thinking for ourselves.

We grow up on music carefully selected to perpetuate our condition. We grow up with a school curriculum carefully selected to keep us from independent thinking. We grow up with television and other film mediums carefully selected to control our view of inferiority. We grow up with foreign religions carefully selected to keep us spiritually bound and prohibiting us from being able to detect deception. One excuse used for this is that these religions actually started in East Africa. The fact still remains that both Christians and Muslims enslaved us and the practice of these religions keep us enslaved. This is just one example of how we make excuses to remain enslaved. Further, it is very irresponsible for preachers to teach us that Christianity is an African religion. This has no basis in reality at all. The Apostle Paul wrote most of the New Testament and he is not African. He is from Turkey. The gospels are based on myths from the Egyptian Book of the Dead, but this is the Egyptian mystery system. This is not Christianity. We will cover more on this topic in the section on religion.

    We should know that our history is mostly from people of the South Atlantic meaning West Africa, the Caribbean, and the southeastern part of North America. We have our own spirituality that includes Animism and pyramid building. In summary, music, film, schooling and religion are the primary sources for the poverty of our mentality. We are unable to determine when we are being deceived and we are unable to assess the scope of the mental damage. In the rare cases wherein, we have a breakthrough in awareness, we still do not have the knowledge or discipline to detoxify our minds. At this time, we do not have the mental scaffolding in place to build a paradigm of liberation. If we decide to do a mental flush, we are not left with anything but vestiges of white supremacy and sanitized black history to work with. This book intends to help solve this problem by offering alternative mental structures through language and logic that supports liberation.

    We will offer an example from DJ Khaled's 2016 album entitled, *Major Key*. For those who are not aware, this album featured *I Got the Keys* with Jay Z and Future, *Holy Key* with Big Sean and Kendrick Lamar and Betty Wright, and *Nas Album Done* with Nas. While we do have great respect for Nas and others, the first video we saw was with DJ Khaled and Nas. It demonstrated no keys whatsoever. *Holy Key* had no spiritual insights at all, although we should give them some credit for trying. *I Got the Keys* was also keyless although we heard that Jay Z was paying bail for some people who may have been wrongfully accused. The following poem is constructive criticism that offers an alternative to what gets played on the radio. It is a poem, not a rap and, of course, there have been other rappers like Dead Prez and Poor Righteous Teachers to offer useful information in their lyrics. Enjoy.

The Real Keys

Keys to what?
  Wealth, survival, unity, happiness,
    Health, harmony, freedom, what?
 How do we come out of this economic
  But also psychological rut?
The perennial wisdom of sages is a key to our survival
  It foretells of our final arrival
There is much that we need to learn
  In order to strategically use what we earn
Live simply so that others may simply live. This is one of the keys
  Rappers, in general, do not know what we need
They tend to perpetuate greed
  Conspicuous consumption is not one of the keys
But sustained boycotts can help us unlock some doors
  As we produce what we need, we can even the score
Significantly reducing the ego is one of the keys to our unification
  Which also enables us to overcome destabilization
Alcohol, half-dressed women, and bling are not part of the solution
Group survival over individual greed
  Must be the basis for developing our institutions
Following stars with expensive cars is not a key to freedom's path

Like yachts with hot tubs and champagne bubble baths
But the rich among us can contribute to controlling our food
   So that when the system crashes, we won't lose
Meanwhile, emulating the oppressor is a brainwashed, hot mess
   But, Mutual Aid Societies are a key to our progress
 Following a crony capitalist system
   Is not a key and does not impress
     The rich get richer, but the masses get less
Buying gold and diamonds from the foreign invader
   Finances our own oppression
A transfer of wealth used to amplify aggression
   Including police repression
Take a self-reflective look at what you are grinding for
   If money really made you happy, why do you always need more?
We have to be clear about the truth
   That is disseminated to our youth
Maintaining rites of passage is a key to our proper growth
   We are making bread and giving it back
     Which is about as useful as burnt toast
Our youth need to know that trinkets are for boys
   A grown man should realize we don't need expensive, shiny toys
This doesn't define our self-worth
   It only sends more youth from the streets to the hearse
They are on the grind trying to find more meaning in life
   Ill-fed and misled following stars with no light
Our youth may want bling
   But they need wisdom that transcends time
   So it is up to the elders to correct the rhymes
Pandering to their greedy, selfish desires for bling
   Is not going to save them
     It will only further degrade them
And encourage them to do unpardonable things
   Just so they can be like the videos with flashy bling bling

We must teach and practice self-discipline toward self-control
  Individually and collectively. That is the goal
The best thing we can do with our money
  Is to unlock the financial chains
A key to our wealth is to alter the rules of the game
  Then we will see some real change
When are we going to start having strategy discussions?
  While we gain wealth and businesses
    We know there will be repercussions
We should know that corporations represent
  The pathological pursuit of profit and power
  Although the documentary on this is more than 2 hours
It is not as long as a sports contest
  Which attracts us and distracts us as we ignore the rest
Stop teaching our children to follow oppressive fools
  Where we are the majority, we must make the rules
Akala said "murder runs the globe", not money
  Highlighting our critical need of defense
But we cannot follow up on this protection
  If all our money is spent
Like China with the Yuan
  We have to recognize the con
What are we doing when we travel overseas?
  International alliances are one of the keys
In order to overcome the detriments of our time
  We need the keys that unlock the chains on our minds
Freedom from European and Jewish domination
  Is the necessary grind
  It is around this theme that we must compose our rhymes
Then we will see light emanate from the stars
  As they truly begin to shine

One of the reasons young blacks do not make revolutionary music is that it will not be played on the radio and, therefore, it is very difficult to make a living with black positive hip hop. Dominant advertisers want us to buy from them, not pull away from them. Most black people are actually afraid of anything revolutionary because of centuries of torture and terrorism that continues to this day. In this poem on *The Real Keys,* we mention the need for defense. It has become clear that we cannot depend on the system in the U.S. to defend us. Quite the opposite is our reality. The so-called justice system offends us rather than defends us as shown by Michelle Alexander in *The New Jim Crow*. Even when we have a black Mayor and black Police Chief, the system still hunts us down to brutalize us, murder us, or lock us away. One cannot get into these leadership positions without demonstrating loyalty to the system that destroys people of color. Ultimately, we will have to find international and domestic means of defending our ability to survive. The next two poems encourage us to defend our physical and mental well-being. They are old poems, but they will be relevant until we are free.

Protect One Another

We are killing ourselves through individualism and greed
   We are not protecting those who are in need
We have to protect our minds, which are our only defense
   When we control our education
     We will understand compensatory recompense
Let's teach unity and harmony
   Rather than individualism and violence
     It is time to speak up rather than remaining silent
We are still confined to mental slavery
   Yet convinced that we have the freedom to learn
     We are blinded by the dollars we earn

Struggle for independence and sovereignty
  Only then can we end poverty
But we do not have the right to be free
  That is not on the agenda in D.C.
They cannot remain wealthy without a poor class
  Nor can they do it without destroying our past
Still, do not be afraid of making demands
  We must have our seeds and we must have our land
The dominant culture does not have our interest at heart
  They have mistreated us from the start
If you think Uncle Sam loves you, then ask for your seeds
  Ask him for the fruits of your deeds
He is only your friend if you do not upset the status quo
  That means we stay on the bottom, you know
If we are cut off from our people, we have no security
  Neither do we have any spiritual purity
Money cannot protect us
  Only unity can protect us
Unity will take the fear out of standing up for survival
  It will enable us to overcome our rivals
Counter-intelligence has paralyzed our resistance
  But ask Curtis Mayfield about persistence
If we stand strong together, we cannot be destroyed
  Perpetual exploitation will be null and void
We must resist acculturation
  We must resist domination
Recognize the times
  Stop exploiting our own people
  With white collar, black on black crime
Protect one another, teach each other
  Including our mothers, fathers, sisters, and brothers

A Clean Mind Is Black

We sell our land to the man on demand
  For some cash in hand
    Not realizing we are being cheated
Unfortunately, our ignorance allows this process
  To be continually repeated
So, we move to the city for some creature comforts
  Then we are still abused, confused, and mistreated
Our terrestrial children are left with no land on which to survive
We have been removed from our connection to God
  So we do not feel the vibe
We have sold our soul to the slaver's path of righteousness
  Which brings us great sorrow
We must understand each culture has its own rituals and
  There are rules to follow when we borrow
Nature is the measuring stick of truth from folly
  We must learn Nature's rules
    Or be tricked by the wooden wand, made from holly
We are still sitting in the temples every Sunday
  Waiting on a foreign savior
It is far past time to check the process
  That creates this behavior
Pseudo-democracy holds us as political prisoners
  But we believe it is the best way
Recognize we can still be hung or jailed or beaten
  Any time of any day
As citizens, we still do not get to vote
  On decisions pertinent to our growth
Education does not teach us to think for ourselves
  Our thoughts are purposely narrowed
We do not see the pyramids in America
  We are too busy focusing on Egyptian Pharaohs

We work all year long and give our income back to the man
   Somehow, we did not grasp in our upbringing
     That money (power) comes from the land
We watch foreign (white) television programs religiously
   Caught up in another man's game
We listen to songs that we know are wrong
   And think that they do not affect our brain
We can recite them in our slanderer's language
   Or at least our children can
Who controls their inputs and guides their thinking?
   Is it us or the man?
We read and write just like the slaver
   But we think for ourselves...right?
This theme calls out to us over and over again
   Because brainwashing is our plight
Where are our spoken languages and writing systems
   That express our God-given minds?
Have we given up on freedom
   Because the information is too hard to find?
Children want to be like their heroes or heroines
   Who are all domesticated blacks
We cannot find images of independent Black Americans
   That is something his story lacks
When we are used up
   They will find another life force
   From which to extract power
If it's not time to talk about the genocidal tricks
   Then tell me - when is the hour?
We are called African-American, but the same logic suggests that
   Everybody is from African evolution
That is not very consistent with reality
   The truth is, there is more than one possible solution
God gave us what we need for self-reliance

But we will have to endure the hardships of non-compliance
Once we have learned the tricks in the enemy's historical science
   Overcoming mind control
     Requires a strong stand of true defiance
A New Black American Order must prevail
  But we must stop them from crushing our efforts
  And sending our prophets to jail
We were not told about the 20-year plan
  But we say nothing about a sin of omission
When the truth is brought to us, we recite in defense
   What we learned from our whitewashed condition
Glorified ignorance is the new black music
  As they make fun of our soul
We are only passing on the enemy's power
  Because our minds are under his control
Surely, high class blacks are not brainwashed like the ghetto child
  We are too intelligent and have too much style
But our comforts and education
   Were designed for us to be "black and mild"
    And our domesticated lifestyle goes back awhile
Strutting around school thinking we were cool
  We were taught how to praise exploitative ways
   Just like the brothers at the labor pool
We are in a degraded and deplorable mental condition
  And this is the reason why we are on an intellectual mission
 It is time to mature in our thinking and get away from being green
  Let these words flow like water to wash our minds clean
Weave the towel in the paths of our thoughts
  And our intellectual life
  For us, a clean mind is a black mind
   No other would be right

We have made it clear that teaching our children about Civil Rights is not the same as teaching them about freedom. While it is true that freedom is a struggle, it is also true that all struggles are not necessarily about freedom. We do not teach our children about how to spot an FBI agent in our organizations, for example. We do not teach them about how to defeat COINTELPRO. We are not telling them what they need to know. We do not teach them how to infiltrate and gather intelligence from those opposed to our liberation. We teach them about being able to vote for a white supremacist or a black person who will maintain the same culture of white supremacists. This is not something to be proud of. This does not make us free mentally, physically, or spiritually. It further legitimizes our perpetual slavery by convincing our youth that the playing field has been leveled, since a black man can become President. We do not teach our children that he is a puppet of the established, oppressive Euro-Jewish order.

Again, Mumia Abu Jamal said that even when we win, we lose. The puppeteers pulling the strings are still giving us the blues. Obviously, the game is rigged. It is rather like a casino. It is set up for us to have fun (lol), but ultimately for us to lose. We have to understand the other (lol), the logic of liberation. Winning a Civil Rights case from time to time, is analogous to winning at the casino jubilantly, but infrequently. If we keep playing this game, we will give our winnings back and inevitably become losers. We are not teaching our children how to win, how to become liberated by not playing the game. As we stop accepting subhuman status, we can work towards becoming fully human. At this time, we are still teaching our children how to be losers even if they make good money. Substantial wealth in the hands of a few does not free us from oppression. It legitimizes oppression. It does not free us anymore than it did Denmark Vesey who won a sum of money, paid for his manumission, and built a successful business. Wealthy black freedom fighters have a history of being destroyed in the U.S. The United States hates freedom. They use an opposite's game to manufacture consent for genocide which they call freedom.

A defensive strategy has to be created in the mind and expressed in the culture. One of the most powerful weapons of creating a mentality of defense is a Mother singing or chanting freedom songs around the house. This often leads to discussions about freedom rather than discussion about the latest propaganda on the news. For black Americans, this does not include Jewish savior songs and Arab desert chants. The following poem/song/chant was written with liberation language in mind. It is a way to remember our freedom fighters and a method of perpetuating resistance even after freedom is won.

Vesey

Denmark Vesey
He let us know
The struggle wouldn't be easy
So let's go
Fighting for the group
Because
We've got to save the youth
We want the children
To all know the truth
Let the people sing
Together we rise
Remember
High as the listening skies
I'm saying
Denmark Vesey
He risked his own precious life

For all of us
To make things right
Inspired by
What happened in Haiti
He decided to
Teach it to the babies
Straight from the pulpit
He knew
That his teaching was legit
I'm saying that
Denmark Vesey
Don't you know that
He was already free
He won a little lottery green
And decided he would buy his freedom clean
But another thing he did know
That old pharaoh had to let his people go
Even though he was a free man
He let many thousands know his plan
Even though he was a wealthy man
He still had demands
He was the original
Yes we can
Obama can't compare
To what Vesey had prepared
I'm saying that
Denmark Vesey
He didn't say I got mine
And complain that black folks whine
Or complain about crabs in a barrel
He aimed so he could shoot a mighty arrow
Yes, he set up a church
Just so he could help heal the hurt

He was an unsung hero
That all black Americans should know
But this is just a preamble
To inspire us to pick up the mantle
To discontinue being fools
And work toward self-rule
Denmark Vesey
He let us know
The struggle wouldn't be easy
But if we want to make our future right
We're going to have to fight, fight, fight
We're going to have to fight not flight
We're going to have to fight, fight, fight

Joining the wealthy capitalist class does not make us free. Our wealth can be taken from us at any time because we are not in control as a group. Our children can be killed with impunity by European aggressors anytime because we are not in control. Or in the case of some famous people, members of your family can be killed. What we like about the Denmark Vesey story/song, however, is that he used his money to work towards freedom individually and collectively. It is a perfect example of exactly what we need to do to overcome oppression. Strategic spending is one of the keys which we will see in another poem. Just in case the reader is unaware, we will mention that Denmark Vesey and Morris Brown were founders of the Emmanuel A.M.E. Church in Charleston, South Carolina where Dylan Roof killed nine people at Bible study. It was built in the tradition of the Free African Society. Both Vesey and Brown were minsters of liberation theology. Although they were reduced to the slaver's religion, they were not sitting around waiting on a Jewish savior to liberate them from inhumane conditions. Religion cannot save you and neither can money; but both can be used strategically to move toward liberation. What is required is that we understand the deception and limitations of both money and religion.

Unsurprisingly, we are having some major problems with monetary strategies. While it is important, the struggle is more than just buying black. The idea is to learn and teach how to be black American mentally and economically. We are very much locked into capitalist framework mentally, spiritually, and physically. Using the capitalist struggle to rise up from the lower class is actually inimical to the freedom struggle. It works against us. Allow me to illustrate. If freedom is your goal, your vision, your end game, then obviously money will be required for you to get there. If money is your goal, your vision, your end game, then freedom is not required for you to get there. We will never get to freedom on the money track. This is a deceptive trick.

The quest for wealth is usually accompanied by usury, selfishness, greed, and other character flaws manifested in unscrupulous behavior. We defer to wealthy people with these traits as if they are superior. We desire to emulate this behavior even though all sages in history have told us this leads to a negative end. These work against the ability to unite and thus work toward freedom. Not only that. The problem is built into the structure of capitalism to exploit the most vulnerable people in society. In other words, slavery is an inherent part of the practice of capitalism. To practice capitalism is to maintain slavery. The profit maximization mantra of capitalism involves squeezing the life blood out of every resource, to include people.

What has this done to humanity? Western Europeans united to create a white race in order to wage a full scale offensive attack of genocide and slavery to steal the resources of the Global South. Together with Jews, they are the ultimate partners in crime, not only in the past, but also now. They were able to gain wealth by mercilessly pushing others down. In the U.S., in particular, we have seen Jews, Koreans, and Arabs follow the invaders path at the expense of the people at the bottom, which are black people. Foreign groups unite and expand economically by exploiting the most vulnerable in society. The American dream is based on the land and labor of natives and displaced Africans. It is a nightmare.

What you will see in the following diagram is how this cannot possibly work for black people. In order for us to rise, we have to exploit the people at the bottom; but those are our own people. Therefore, it is divisive rather than cohesive and elevating. By design, we cannot unify and build capitalist wealth as other groups have done. We are kept out of the loop. There is not another group beneath us to extract wealth from. Therefore, we will have to reject the normal working of capitalism, which is to say reject slavery in the process of planning for freedom. We will have to create a different paradigm than the one we are locked into. In order to affect liberation in this area, we will share another crude diagram followed by a poem. Some people are visual learners, so we want this information to be accessible to everyone.

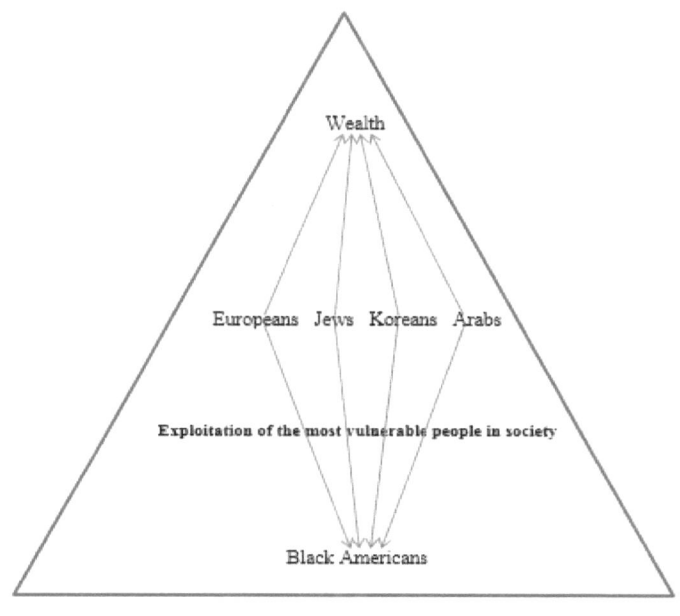

Capitalist Pyramid

Out of the LUEP

LUEP is an acronym for Little Understood Economic Phenomenon
  We are still going through life with Euro-Jewish blinders on
Other cultures can unify to exploit blacks
  In a full-scale economic attack
Europeans, Koreans, Arabs, and Jews
  Repeatedly, unabashedly we continue to be abused
But we cannot unify to exploit these groups
  Because we are on the bottom tier
    So how can we come up from here?
Capitalism exploits the most vulnerable in society
  Business as usual, immorality, and impropriety
So, when we succumb to joining this destructive force
  We end up exploiting and trampling
    On our own people, of course
Therefore, capitalism can be unifying for other peoples
  But divisive for blacks
Because whomever comes up, steps on the poor
  Where we are stuck in a self-defeating trap
The better part of reason suggests that we use a different approach
  That supports unified gains
Rather than greedily exploiting our own
  Which ensures that oppression stays the same
Mutual Aid Societies are one such solution
  If we can just clean out some of our mental pollution
This is about loving, caring, and sharing
  That would keep us from marching in circles
  And help us get our bearing
In lieu of the selfishness, usury, and deception
  That has kept us enslaved and repressed
    Since capitalism's inception
This poem is to stimulate our minds

To enable us to think outside of the box
Even trapped in an open air prison
  Our creativity can pick the locks
Capitalism empowers us with the fantasies of becoming rich
And we might die trying to get there
  While freedom remains a myth
This economic system shows us how to steal
  Not how to fulfill
    Let's keep it real
Cooperative economics is a start
  But unified economics is even better
Cease and desist with boxed in capitalism
  Our approach has to be unfettered
I'm saying, limitless creativity must be at the heart
  To get us moving in a solution-oriented direction
    Liberation language is my part

We are essentially trying to reverse the genocide and get out of the pet stage of slavery. This is not the Denmark Vesey time of slavery. This is a much worse mental situation in which, we do not even want to be free. We also think Euro-Jewish power is greater than any God we could summon. That is the pet stage of bondage. Slaves want to be free. Pets do not want to be free. Pets want to be pleasing, accepted, and loved. Most of our people are pets of the dominator. We want to be just like the blue bloods that are destroying the planet. This happens to educated and uneducated blacks. Conspicuous wealth does not change pet status. This describes a rich pet. Most people have seen the lavish accommodations that rich people set up for their pets? They especially like pets/people who entertain them. We will not elaborate because that is going to step on a lot of toes. If you are apathetic about becoming free of European and Jewish domination, then you are a pet. If you are fraught with a defeatist mentality that believes we cannot ever become free, then you are like a zoo animal. Harriet Tubman is reported to have dealt with this same issue in her day. She said that she could have freed more if they knew they were slaves. Given the number of slave revolts that occurred during her time, it is unlikely that our downtrodden forbears were unaware of their situation. We are going to share another Harriet Tubman poem in light of a discussion about putting her likeness on the money. We will follow it with poems that are to help us come past an apathetic vibration.

Twenty Dollar Bill

I want to talk a little bit about Harriet Tubman and revolution
  In light of 2016 smoke and mirrors
    That commemorates an illusion
You see, the revolution of a wheel
  Means that it has turned all the way around
    Meaning we are right back where we started
      Quite the opposite of Moses when the sea was parted
You know, he walked through on dry land to get to the other side
  So that he could be free and stay alive
Like from Harriet Tubman's slave state of Maryland
  To the other side
  The racist state of Pennsylvania
    Not unlike the blood suckers of Transylvania
Because we are still caught up in the same vicious empire
  Bob Marley said Babylon system is a vampire
Harriet Tubman may grace the front of the $20 bill
  But Andrew Jackson will still be on the other side
    To remind us of continued genocide
      Keeping the nightmare of global domination alive
She took people from plantation slavery
  To unemployment, or low wages maybe

And we call this freedom...really
   They dropped a bomb on Move in Philly
Do you remember back in 1985
   There is only one of the two survivors still alive
Ask her about revolution
   Ask Ramona Africa about freedom, about solutions
Revolution is taking us right back where we started
   Ask Mumia Abu Jamal
     About how he got trapped behind Pennsylvania prison walls
But we are supposed to believe
   That Harriet Tubman helped those in need
     To find a place of freedom
Come on now, what we accept of this word
   Is ridiculous and absurd
Its deceptive and insidious use
   Is never defined this way for other groups
The Revolutionary War left white folks with land
   World War II left Jews with land
While Harriet Tubman's travels to Philadelphia
   Left us still subjected to the man... and without a freedom plan
It's not a stepping stone
   If you are not working towards getting your own
She was unquestionably brave
   But she didn't free any slaves
In fact, this story locks us into perpetual servitude
   Such that we are still terrorized and abused
Intellectually confused
   As our soul music revolved into rhythm and blues
And it's still controlled externally by Europeans and Jews
   Shucking and jiving as someone else's muse
     Stuck in self-defeating patterns that make us lose
We know the church is slave teachings
   But we are still sitting in the pews

We know mainstream TV is propaganda
  But we're still watching the news
Listening to misleading rhetoric
  About Harriet Tubman being on the $20 bill
    People get real
We wouldn't know reality if it slapped us in the face
  As we are falling for the ideology that we are all one race
Predator and prey
  Dr. King made it clear that we are still not free today
Predators are hunting us down and killing us every 28 hours
  Tell me again how freedom is defined
    While we are languishing, anguishing without any real power
Freedom is not about running away from slavery
  Into another system of the same damn people
    Hoping and praying that they might treat us as equals
Freedom is not an integration fight
  Where we are marching and begging for Civil Rights
As Malcolm X helped us understand
  Freedom is always about land
I am not talking about 40 acres and a mule
  That can be taken right back
    In a state sponsored Ku Klux Klan style attack
What Harriet Tubman did was amelioration
  Not liberation
This requires that we take it up a couple of notches
  Set the bar a little higher
    Liberation requires that we come out of the fire
Into a place where we can practice the wisdom of old
  Freedom land is a place where we can defend
    Our spiritual and economic control
The slavery to freedom story is only real
  When we can decide who goes on the $20 bill

Apathy

Apathy is when we don't care enough
  About ourselves and our children
    To find out what is really going on
Apathy is when we don't stand together
  So that we can stand strong
Apathy is allowing our movements to be limited at every turn
  Controlled in what we do and what we earn
Made possible because the perpetrator
  Has countless stolen loot to burn
Apathy is when we don't follow the money trail
  To find out why our political prisoners rot in jail
Apathy is when we scurry to the schoolhouse
  Without offering resistance, so that we are still being miseducated
    Dedicated to being degraded
      And psyched out when we think we have made it
Apathy is when life passes us by
  On the television or telephone screen
    Apathy is when we don't know what apathy means
Apathy is when we don't care
  About what religion our ancestors taught
    Before slaves were being sold and bought
I know I stepped on some toes then
  But only because apathy won't let truth in
Apathy is coming from the Ivy League
  Amped up with arrogance and greed
And yet watching people suffer without assistance
  Who are the most in need
Apathy is never being accountable for our condition
  Apathy is lazy, misguided belief in superstitions
Apathy is coming from the ghetto and never going back
  Apathy is not waging meaningful defense

Against the invader's attack
Apathy is forgetting where you come from
  And not understanding where you are
    Apathy pulls up your roots and plants them afar
From Mississippi to Chi-town
  Because strange fruit is hanging all around
Lynching black people so the man can have the land
  Apathy allows this to go on without taking a stand
Apathy is not considering indigenous persons
  And then wondering why our situation has worsened
Apathetic people do not meditate
  Apathetic people are reactionary and too late
But they do celebrate... anything but truth and freedom
  And they are seldom there when you need 'em
Apathy is when you only think about yourself
  And that becomes your new way to wealth
Simply leaving the group behind
  So the individual can shine
But like a black star in the sky
  Apathy is when you don't ask why
Apathy is when you only want a piece of the pie, but not the recipe
  I am trying to offer you the best of me
    To help us overcome the crippling effects of apathy
Before global famine comes
  Because we are too apathetic and numb
  To create our own place in the sun
We cannot afford to let apathy ride
  Understand the consequence of apathy is continued genocide
So, it's time to swallow our pride
  And put apathy aside
Because
  Freedom lives when apathy dies

Reasons to Care

If we are just following the herd and really don't care
   We will continue living in the same nightmare
Ignoring useful information that is freely shared
   Unwilling to upset the status quo because we are lazy or scared
Apathy causes our judgement to become impaired
   Leaving us vulnerable to becoming ensnared
By a system that leaves us terrorized and confused
   Oppression has become so normalized
     That we don't even recognize when we are being abused
We think we are too cool for it to happen to us
   In ignorance we trust
We think we can make it as individuals without group ties
   Until a family member is murdered by police
     That makes us think otherwise
We don't understand the conditions to which we are subjected
   We live with an illusion of feeling protected
Knowledge of self is not on our radar
   We just want a big house and a German car
Unaware that our consumption finances our own demise
   As we refuse to listen to those who are wise
We are playing Russian roulette with a full clip
   And one in the chamber
     Without ever realizing that we are in mortal danger
Now, this doesn't have to inspire anger
   But it should open your mind and start to change 'ya
While we worry about social media and material things
   Nightmares lurk at the edge of our dreams
The elders told us to keep our eyes on the prize
   But our inattention has allowed the trickster
     To change it to illusions and lies
This should come as no surprise

As we go through life with material blinders on our eyes
   Do we want to be second class citizens all of our lives?
Having to work harder and harder to make ends meet
   Risking prison and death for credibility in the street
Our vision is hazy
   Because our hormones are going crazy
     And our minds are lazy
If we really want to make our success stick
   We better pay close attention and learn the tricks
Because our survival is at stake
   We could end up being the victims 'again'
   Of making America great
Knowledge of self is the most important thing we can learn
   Of far greater significance than the money we earn
Our property can be seized and our money taken away
   But if we have the knowledge, we can turn it into a brighter day
If we ever want to see a real change
   We are going to respect people who help us train our brains
So that we can learn to see the game behind the game
   Where age old deception is laid plain
We are not talking about old school or new school
   We are talking about information
     That won't have us out there looking like fools
Together we rise, but divided we fall
   It behooves us to wake up to this knowledge call
Because only then can we become all we can be
   I am not much into drama, but that's my T

We are not making any intellectual progress because we are still being schooled by the same people from 100 years ago. We are stuck in the box, marching in circles. We keep going from trick to trick like the hero twins in Xibalba. The virus mutates and takes away our progress. It is not surprising that we become apathetic or ambivalent. Our pet-like emotions want to stay with the master. We have health insurance and we are feeling a sense of security. But we know deep inside ourselves that we have to fight for freedom in order to survive. Let us be clear. There is no future in joining a virus. The trade-off of survival for temporary comfort is genocide. It is our firm conviction that we need to continue to call the problem what it is until we can get it solved, genocide. William Patterson and his cohorts put together a document in 1951 entitled, *We Charge Genocide*.

The intention was to take this to the United Nations and elsewhere to solicit some help with the inhumanity of European aggression in the U.S. The United States has always been the leader in Human Rights violations. Hitler was a girl scout in comparison. In a recent comparison, greedy Euro-Jewish interests are benefiting from the deaths of over six million people in the Congo. This is only one of many that span the entire globe. Unfortunately, countless years of terrorism has discouraged black American leaders from thinking seriously about defense. This climate made it easy for them to sever their international ties as part of the deal to get Civil Rights legislation passed. The leaders that let the fire of connectivity burn out ignored that Malcolm X said any struggle for freedom in the U.S. that does not include international alliances is doomed to fail. Well, that is still true today. Fortunately, there is a group of young people who are keeping the knowledge of the real problem alive. Of course, they get no media covered because their resistance is not scripted. They chose, appropriately, not to reinvent the wheel and call their organization We Charge Genocide.

We do not know what this group is doing at this time. Their efforts are kept in the dark while Black Lives Matter (BLM) gets the spotlight as they continue in the tradition of marching in circles. That is not to say that they have not done some good work and affected some change. We only mean to reiterate that it is imperative that we have a clear vision of the end game. We are talking about freedom, not equality. We are talking about developing a "never again" strategy, not worrying about the benevolence of the perpetrators. We would also like to comment on the (BLM) slogan in general. As mentioned, there was no need to reinvent the wheel. Sticking with the slogan of We Charge Genocide keeps the adversary from being able to easily dilute the resistance with All Lives Matter or co-opt the resistance with Blue Lives Matter. It makes us wonder if (BLM) is scripted resistance. We have several poems that cover the few topics in this section. We will start with a call and response poem which is written to be interactive with an audience, but I am sure you will get the idea. It speaks to the importance of the slogans used in the struggle. Then we will move on to a poem about our thesis of self-control.

Slogans to Freedom Chants

After exposure of extreme police violence
  Let's look at some slogans we've been given
  It occurs to me that freedom chants are still inaccessibly hidden
Kept from the vision of our movements
  As if liberation is forbidden
For example:
Hands up, don't shoot
  Begging for mercy is at the root
    Like we're all thieves with stolen loot
Or
Black lives matter
  But those in charge couldn't care less
  As long as their pockets get fatter
    The slogan becomes idle chatter
Or
I can't breathe

This doesn't set us at ease
  While they are still choking the life out of our seeds
Or
We charge genocide
  This has already been tried
The foreign invader might change the game
  But he won't actually compromise
Check it...
We need more meaningful slogans to change the situation
  That lead toward self-reliance and protecting our own nation
In order to truly turn things around
  We need the call and response
    From our own cultural background
Calling: Blacks must survive
Responding: By any means necessary
  Healing the wounds of mental fatalism
    Like an old-school apothecary
Calling: The black community
Responding: With common unity
  Let's stop pretending that we're blessed
    Unity, not money, is the key to success
      To overcome this deadly mess
Another chant that might help us overcome our plight
  And encourage more respect for life
Call: Black pride
Response: Stay alive
  Of course, this is reminiscent of James Brown's
Call: Say it loud
Response: I'm black and I'm proud
  Or getting right down to the seed
    Where there is obviously a great need
Call: Save the group
Response: Protect the youth

Or the familiar
Call: No justice
Response: No peace
  A simple chant to help slow down the police
But let's not let these slogans become tautological
  As we remember most of the struggle is psychological
Call: Psych war
Response: Effective no more
  Togetherness is our might
    Enabling us to put up a winning fight
Call: Stay black
Response: Fight back
  We do this by building on successes of the past
    Making sure that our movements last
Call: What's the cause?
Response: Make our own laws
  We have to make sure our people are well-schooled
    Where we are the majority, we must make the rules
Call: What's on your mind?
Response: Policing our own kind
  In order to mitigate violent aggression
    We have to do something about the structure of repression
If we want to win, we have to stay focused until the end
  With defense in place that enables us to say, "Never Again"
To make it clear for the long haul, resound the
Call: What's the goal?
Response: Self control

Self-control

We have story tellers, rappers, singers, and poets
  Giving us their best
    In a freedom quest

But this just helps to numb the pain
   Like cocaine
We take in misinformation and deception like cheap wine
   In order to solve this problem, freedom has to be defined
We have to make sure the right stories told
   Our children and elders have to know
     That freedom is... self-control
And this should be taught in all our sports
   Of course
     How else are we going to get off this horse?
Galloping to the end of blackness
   In a downward spiral
     While we are stuck in stubborn denial
About our own habits and practice
   As we are programmed to self-destruct
     Most of us act like we don't give a fizzuck
The path to reverse genocide
   Is with self-love and self-pride
Not by waiting on black leaders
   To lead us up a self-aware, self-sufficient, self-controlled path
Because that is not happening
   We are tired and still mired in genocidal aftermath
We are going to have to make sure the right stories are told
   Freedom is self-control
Obviously, self-control requires self-discipline
   Very few people are disciples of discipline
But if we are fed up with exploitation and oppression
   We should get the impression
That we are worthy as a group to survive and compete
   So that our lives can become more fulfilled and complete
Except that we run from group think
   Like her breath stinks
Yet it is imperative that we engage in more dialogue

Not monologue
 Because we've got to get this drain unclogged
Malignant piping that holds our energy captive
 Until we are unable to breathe
  This deadly virus that infects the people came from overseas
Now, they've gone global
 Controlling mediums that make it seem noble
The problem mostly infects the Global South
 Destroying healthy cells and creating no way out
The prospects for our future are dire
 In this stressed at the seams, out of control, empire
There is a specific culture of attack on all areas of black lives
 Including the colluding with black agents and spies
We sell each other out for money that was created out of thin air
 And to make matters worse, we don't even care
 Allowing for the growth of destabilization
  Which is more than just misinformation
That puts the invader on a pinnacle up above
 While simultaneously destroying black love
Destroying unity
 With impunity
  Designed to permanently weaken you and me
So, we have to make sure the right stories are told
 Freedom is self-control
We have to define freedom for ourselves
 Then we can determine whether we are living well
  Upon close examination, something begins to smell
Like the hunters who hunt us down
 Or the policies that jerk us around
  Examples abound
We are tired of the lies that never surprise
 We are tired of domination in whatever disguise
We have been told many times

That we have to produce rather than consume
   And this is still the elephant in the room
We have been told to buy black
   But we cannot seem to accomplish that
We have been told to go to church
   After 150 years, that still doesn't work
Then we act like we don't know
   That slave worship is just sucking up to the status quo
We have been told to fight for legal rights
   Yet there is still no freedom in sight
We have black Mayors and Police Chiefs
   Still no relief
Because they move to the beck and call of the dominant group
   And continue to incessantly terrorize our youth
Who are shucking and jiving to self-destructive grooves
   By now, we should be picking up on the clues
Self-control definitely requires self-restraint
   It seems simple and straight forward, but it ain't
Everything in this society
   Is designed to overcome our ability to resist
     Which ensures that our subservient condition persists
Freedom is not just new laws
   Freedom is a new cause
A worthy cause that doesn't manipulate us into circular gains
   While we still feel the pain
Of domination by our own elites
   Who ensure our defeat
     By perpetuating the same system, marching to the same beat
Emulating the oppressor is not self-control
   And we need to be careful with how these stories are being told
We must understand that our place and our role
   Is not to be dominated by foreigners
     Freedom is self-control

And one for Marcus Garvey

Black Star Line

Let's have a revival of the Black Star Line
  For the survival of the Black American kind
These won't be slave ships
  On the contrary, these will be freedom ships
That encourage us to work on ourselves
  Then on our relationships
To help us rise above the tumultuous waters of oppression
  By making thoughts of freedom an obsession
In order to carry us to the shores of liberty
  Through restoring our southern Atlantic identity
Survival compels us to claim independence
  From foreign domination
    Rather than joining in the wealth stealing of a genocidal nation
As we learn to float above the high tides of distraction
  That keeps us from progressing with liberating actions
Weakening modern technology
  Has been doing less good and more harm
  As our people become an endangered species
  And we are not even alarmed
We carry on as if the dominant culture
  Will always take care of our needs
We are drowning in our ignorance
  As we ignore facts for what we believe
We are sailing into the future with our slave mentality
  That we learned in school, in society... and in church
A few token Negroes make a little more money
  And we don't realize things are getting worse
The freedom ship is docked and anchored
  From a current of temporary prosperity

While the raiders continue to rob the ship
  With precision and regularity
We can no longer fill the vessel with rations
  Because we have lost control of our food supply
    Coerced into moving to the city to get a bigger piece of the pie
We have been tricked into navigating the seas
  Guided by celebrities and other fake stars
    As we are emotionally misled
      About where we are going and who we are
The freedom ship will have to remind us
  Of our true southern Atlantic history
Beyond the popular Mediterranean Sea
  And East African mysteries
We have to learn about our origins from a west side perspective
  And we'll see why our knowledge of self
    Has heretofore been ineffective
We learn about pyramids in Egypt, but not in Illinois
  Because we are too busy and distracted
    With our trinkets and toys
Trying to fill an empty void that used to give birth to fire
  With uncompromising reasons to overcome the empire
Like the steam ships of Marcus Garvey
  We have to rekindle the flames
To give us the energy
  To sail above an ocean of illusions and games
We have to recognize when the winds are changing
  And we are blown off course
And not be misguided by fake black leaders as a navigation source
Constructing freedom vessels
  Will keep us from sailing into the abyss
As we look to the heroes in our communities
  To help us with this
On our Elusive Quest for Freedom that we can never seem to find

Like a phoenix from the ashes
Let's revive the Black Star Line

Europeans, especially in the U.S. have brought us to the brink of nuclear and ecological disaster. We have to be able to envision a future where the European diaspora are no longer dominating the Global South with hyper-aggressive violence. Anything resembling an attempt at equality means that so-called white people will have to learn to live without stealing from other people and exploiting their labor. Equality means that white people will only be in charge of white people. Other people will have autonomous control of their own resources and livelihood with an equal ability to defend themselves. Equality may never happen, but we can certainly define it appropriately, so we can grasp the reality of the possibility. We can swing the pendulum in that direction. Our survival does not depend on equality, but it does depend on us developing a "never again" strategy. We want the definition of equality which means that white people will never again be in charge of black people or any other people in the Global South.

Never Again

The overwhelming, all-encompassing aggression of the invader
  Leaves us almost without defense
Outnumbered and outgunned
  Unable to bring about meaningful recompense
Teachers unions and police unions
  Will not bow down to community oversight
    We'll have to work from the bottom-up to overcome our plight
Let unity be our dynamite
  To blast our way into a fair fight
Something we can win
  Something that will enable to say, "Never again"

Never again is when we are no longer taken away from our places
  As if we have fallen outside of God's graces
    And forgotten that the struggle is all about races
Never again is when we stop falling prey
  To the manacles of injustice
    The revolution can be bloodless
When we swallow ego and pride to look inside
  And find ways to trust this
Never again is when we believe in ourselves, invest in ourselves
  Overcoming oppressive hell
    Learning to just say no to being locked away in slave cells
Never again is when we stop allowing ourselves to be dominated
  Stopping the nonsense of trying to become integrated
    Into a society in which we have always been hated
Never again is when we are not
  Governed by a foreign people for profit
In spite of greedy self-haters who will try to knock it
  We have to develop creative ways to stop it
Never again will we be economically disenfranchised
  While each generation seems to be surprised
Because we still haven't produced what we need
  For our black lives
Never again is when black lives matter enough to produce
  Sustenance for our souls and defense against abuse
When we care enough about people
  To become the head and not the caboose
Never again is when we disallow
  Caricatures and misrepresentations
    On the radio and television stations
Overcoming misinformation
  By controlling its dissemination to our black nation
Never again is when we are no longer tricked

By medical experiments
  Where biological warfare works to our detriment
Teachers and healers must plan
  To counter spin these impediments
Never again will we accept the foreign religion game
  Received and believed because of terrorism and pain
  As we move into freedom, truth will be made plain
Never again will we follow hierarchical systems
  Of inequity and iniquity
In all walks of life with inescapable ubiquity
  Leaving the police to stop and frisk me
    To take away our dignity
Never again will we be without resourceful land
  Having to depend on employment from the invader
    Known as the pale man
We can provide for our own
  As we unify, plan, and take a stand
Never again will we be without a defense strategy
  That protects our group
"By any means necessary" is hard philosophy to refute
  Because we will need to use all of our most thoughtful attributes
Never again will we join the most aggressive military on the planet
  Taking the causes of invasion for granted
  Pretending that we don't know every operation is underhanded
Never again will we be controlled by fear
  We hold the future of our lives dear
    Perpetual resistance in all forms is the only way to survive here
Never again will we be tricked out of independence for blacks
  As we are spiritually, mentally and physically attacked
  We will never ever give up on freedom. Run tell that.

What this poem attempts to demonstrate is that if our political strategy is not a "never again" strategy, then it cannot lead us toward survival. Consider another people whose survival was threatened. The mistreatment of Jews led to a "never again" strategy which not only includes land, but most likely includes a significant stockpile of nuclear weapons which no organization is allowed to inspect or count or regulate. Hypocritically, they want to denuclearize every Muslim country around them. This is classic asymmetrical domination. It is hard to tell whether they took a page from the U.S. book of hegemony or if they actually wrote it. Either way, we have a human right to develop an even better "never again" strategy than Israel since we have been treated far worse than they can ever imagine. But in order to pull our energy into working for their survival instead of our own, they program us with movies like *The Matrix*. It is all about protecting Zion. Israel, led by Zionists, intends to be the last country standing. Meanwhile, the genocide of black Americans continues to this day. It has not even been curbed by Dr. King's strategy of non-violence. So, we have to find ways to take away his ability to drive us into extinction.

Take away his ability

External control physically, mentally and spiritually
  Is still the primary problem
    We know who is sticking it to us, but how can we stop them?
We have been complaining about the same issues
  Since I was born in the 1960s
    After 50 years of struggle, they can still stop and frisk me
In order to overcome this crisis
  We have to implement a better way to fight this
We have to take away the oppressor's ability to do these things
  If we ever expect to hear freedom ring

Marching with cameras and celebrities

Will not take away his ability
Raising awareness to the same problems over and over
　Cannot take away his ability
Voting for hand-picked candidates will not take away his ability
　Remaining inside a dominated political apparatus
　　Cannot take away his ability
Entrepreneurship will not take away his ability
　Media ownership cannot take away his ability
More assimilated miseducation will not take away his ability
　Better schools with the same curriculum
　　Cannot take away his ability
Belief in foreign religions will not take away his ability
　Tithing and Ramadan cannot take away his ability
Pyramids in Egypt will not take away his ability
　African consciousness cannot take away his ability
Knowledge of melanin will not take away his ability
　The pineal gland or third eye cannot take away his ability
The best of entertainment will not take away his ability
　Wealthy actors and athletes cannot take away his ability
More jobs for the poor will not take away his ability
　Raising minimum wage cannot take away his ability
All of these tactics are inadequate
　Because they cannot and will not take away his ability

It is important to pursue these things to ameliorate our condition
　But we must not lose sight of the prize
Only a complete and fully committed struggle for sovereignty
　Will enable the masses to rise
Liberation on all fronts will take away his control
　But we have to want sovereign control deep down in our soul
Continuously organized and implemented boycotts
　Will take away his ability
Stopping the consumption of all luxury goods

Can take away his ability
Seceding from his political domination will take away his ability
   Rewriting the rules of local politics can take away his ability
Reconnecting oppressed rich with oppressed poor
   Will take away his ability
Replacing capitalism with participatory economics
   Can take away his ability
Creating autonomous, self-reliant public education
   Will take away his ability
Developing our own police academies
   Can take away his ability
Departing from the oppressor's religion
   Will take away his ability
The Southern Atlantic spiritual heritage can take away his ability
   Understanding that our identity begins in America
     Will take away his ability
Knowing our sovereign future in this land can take away his ability
   Making a commitment to unity will take away his ability
Solving the unique problems of the 13% can take away his ability
   Turning off the radio and television will take away his ability
Liberating internet edutainment can take away his ability
   Working in community gardens will take away his ability
Taking control of our resources can take away his ability
   Controlling our own cryptocurrencies can take away his ability

We can build micro houses together with those without homes
   We can restore human dignity to those left alone
We can buy water rights for the future of our most basic needs
   We must integrate survivability and sustainability
     Into what we believe
We should be developing solar power for the people of the south
   This will give us an advantage and a way to come out
Coming from under oppressive dominance

Should be our unified goal
But we have to want sovereign control deep down in our soul

Transition to Volume Two

We have known for some time that we have to use our knowledge and skills for our own benefit rather than having our mental and physical skills exploited by a foreign invading group who intend to extract wealth from us indefinitely. The problem to solve is to take away the ability of the aggressor to continue to use and abuse us at will. We can determine empirically what kind of unity, resources, and allegiances that would be necessary to break free from the control of bloodsuckers that suck the labor and life out of black Americans and people of the Global South generally. As we continue with the language of murderers, it becomes more and more difficult to conceptualize peace and harmony. It becomes obvious that we have to deal with the problem of language in order for math and science to do us any good as a group.

Let us consider some language from one of the greatest writers of the 20th century. One useful way to transition to volume two is to unpack a quote from James Baldwin's, *The Fire Next Time*. "I have met only a very few people - and most of these were not Americans - who had any real desire to be free. Freedom is hard to bear. It can be objected that I am speaking of political freedom in spiritual terms, but the political institutions of any nation are always menaced and are ultimately controlled by the spiritual state of that nation. We are controlled here by our confusion, far more than we know, and the American dream has therefore become something much more closely resembling a nightmare…"

The first topic of Baldwin's quote has to do with freedom. In trying to solve the problem of perpetual slavery, we have to deal with the fact that black Americans are largely in the pet stage of slavery. Pets don't want to be free. Given this context, we have tried to appeal to our sense of survivability, sustainability, dignity, and morality in an attempt to open our minds to the necessity of freedom. Our terms have been defined with careful clarity so as to provide a unifying foundation for our struggle of sovereign humanity.

The second topic from Baldwin speaks to our spiritual world view. In this volume, some conversation was initiated about the spiritual state of our black American nation. At this point, we should at least know the difference between indigenous spirituality and foreign invader's spirituality. This parallels an understanding of a constructive mental state vs. a destructive mental state. Spirituality will be more explicitly covered in volume two. Again, we will define and clarify in a way that we hope will inspire some people to desire freedom. As inferred by Baldwin's quote, spiritual freedom is inextricably linked to political-economic freedom.

The third topic from Baldwin is confusion. For the third time, our strategy has been to define and clarify. For example, we introduced a diagram of the political left and right. This illustration served to offer an undeniable view of our political impotence. The same diagram, however, illustrates the end game and offers a visual representation of what we call freedom, defined as self-control. This helps us to clear up lingering confusion. We are easily deceived and confused when we are not grounded in indigenous spirituality. These are directly connected.

Baldwin finishes with a comment about the American dream resembling a nightmare. Let us be clear that the American dream has always been Manifest Destiny and its extension of global Domination. We illustrated this nightmare in a crude diagram called Going Viral. We have to plan for the level of merciless aggression that we are up against when deception no longer works in their favor. This book intends to open our eyes to the deception, violence, and greed that we will have to overcome in order to succeed as a group. In other words, it is a wakeup call enabling us to emerge from the dream world into a waking reality of survivability as a group.

We have been recording problems with foreign invasion and domination for decades. We have not adequately grasped the severity or gravity of the problems partially because we are using the same world view and language. We have to take away the invader's spiritual world view and his use of language in order to take away his ideology of exploitation. Recently, we learned from *The New Jim Crow* by Michelle Alexander. Before that, we learned form *We Charge Genocide* by William Patterson. An earlier work was *Miseducation of the Negro* by Carter G. Woodson.

The perennial problem with miseducation can be dealt with using Neely Fuller Jr.'s idea of creating a compensatory counter-racist code which can also establish a mutually beneficial relationship among victims of destabilization. As with all mammals, most of what we learn is taught. Rather than teaching a state-mandated curriculum designed to maintain the status quo; we should be teaching a compensatory counter-racist code. Education is the cornerstone of any serious struggle for freedom. We start volume two with education.

References

Books:

Abram, David. *Spell of the Sensuous*. Vintage Books. 1996

Acuna, Rodolfo. *Occupied America: The Chicano's Struggle Toward Liberation*. Canfield Press. 1972

Aharone, Ezra. *Pawned Sovereignty*. 1st Books. 2003

Albert, Michael. *Practical Utopia: Strategies for a Desirable Society*. PM Press. 2017

Alexander, Michelle. *The New Jim Crow*. The New Press. 2012

Anderson, Claud. *PowerNomics*. PowerNomics Corporation of America. 2001

Budge, E.A. Wallis. *Egyptian Book of the Dead*. Dover Publications 1967

Carew, Jan. *Rape of Paradise: Columbus and the Birth of Racism in the Americas*. A and B Distributors. 1994

Caruthers, Jacob. *Intellectual Warfare*. Third World Press. 1999

Chomsky, Noam. *Hegemony or Survival: America's Quest for Global Dominance*. Holt. 2003

Chomsky, Meyer, and Alvarado. *New World of Indigenous Resistance*. City Lights Books. 2010

Churchill, Ward and Vander Wall, Jim. *Agents of Repression: The FBIs Secret War Against the Black Panther Party and the American Indian Movement*. South End Press. 1990

Easterly, William. *The Elusive Quest for Growth: Economists' Adventures and Misadventures in the Tropics.* Mit Press. 2001

Ferguson, Charels H. *Predator Nation.* Crown Business. 2012

Freire, Paulo. *Pedagogy of the Oppressed.* Bloomsbury Academic. 1968

Fuller, Neely. *The United Independent Compensatory Code/System/Concept: A Compensatory Counter-Racist Code.* Neely Fuller, Jr. 1957-2016

Gatto, John Taylor. *Dumbing Us Down.* New Society Publishers. 1992

Gillen, Jay. *Educating for Insurgency.* AK Press. 2014

Hahnel, Robin. *Economic Justice and Democracy.* Taylor and Francis Group. 2005

Hale, Annie Riley. *A School Ma'am Looks at Money.* San Pasqual Press. 1940

Healing BALM . *Elusive Quest for Freedom.* Huaca Enterprises. 2010

Horne, Gerald. *Black Revolutionary: William Patterson and the Globalization of the African American Freedom Struggle.* University of Illinois Press. 2013

Horne, Gerald. *The Counter Revolution of 1776: Slave Resistance and the Origins of the United States of America.* New York University Press. 2014

Illich. Ivan. *Deschooling Our Society.* Marion Boyars. 1970

Klein, Naomi. *The Battle for Paradise*. Haymarket Books. 2018

Klein, Naomi. *The Shock Doctrine: The Rise of Disaster Capitalism*. Picador. 2007

Machiavelli, Niccolo. *The Prince*. The University of Chicago Press. 1998

Marcus, Bruce and Taber, Michael, editors. *Maurice Bishop Speaks: The Grenada Revolution 1979-83*. Pathfinder Press. 1983

Nation of Islam. *The Secret Relationship Between Black and Jews*. Latimer Associates. 1991

Patterson, William. *We Charge Genocide: The Crime of Government Against the Negro People*. International Publishers Co. 3rd ed. 2017

Perkins, John. *Confessions of an Economic Hit Man*. Plume. 2004

Sale, Kirkpatrick. *Conquest of Paradise: Christopher Columbus and the Columbian Legacy*. Plume 1990

Smith, Charles Hugh. *A Radically Beneficial World: Automation, Technology, and Creating Jobs for All.* Oftwominds. 2015

Smith, Phillip B. and Max-Neef, Manfred. *Economics Unmasked*. Green Books. 2011

Steptoe, John. *Mufaro's Beautiful Daughters*. Lothrop, Lee and Shepard Books. 1987

Tedlock, Dennis. *Popol Vuh*. Simon and Schuster. 1985

Welsing, Dr. Frances Cress. *The Cress Theory of Color Confrontation and Racism (White Supremacy) (A Psycho-Genetic Theory and World Outlook)*. C-R Publishers 13th ed. 1989

Wilder, Craig Steven. *Ebony and Ivy*. Bloomsbury Press. 2013

Woodson, Carter G. *Miseducation of the Negro*. The Associated Publishers. 1933

Videos:

All Wars are Banker's Wars. By Michael Rivero. Whatreallyhappened.com. 2015

The Corporation. Directed by Mark Achbar and Jennifer Abbott. Written by Joel Bakan. 2003

First Americans Were Black Aborigines. BBC. 2012
The Illegitimacy of a People Called Jews. Spoken by Pastor Ray Hagins. 2011

Inception. Directed and written by Christopher Nolan. 2010

Kite Runner. Directed by Marc Forster. Screenplay by David Benioff. 2007

Life and Debt. Directed by Stephanie Black. Written by Jamaica Kincaid. 2001

Money Masters. Directed by William T. Still. Written by Patrick Carmack and William T. Still. 1996

The Panama Deception. Directed by Barbara Trent. Written by David Kasper. 1992

The Power of Community: How Cuba Survived Peak Oil. Directed by Faith Morgan. 2006

The Matrix. Directed and Written by the Wachowski brothers. 1999

Tale of the Forgotten People Of Andaman Island - Jarawa Tribe Documentary. 2017

Why You Cannot Have a Capitalist Democracy. Noam Chomsky. 2014

Websites:

Ball, Norman. *The Cancer Thinks it's the Body Politic*. July 22, 2018. https://dissidentvoice.org/2018/07/the-cancer-thinks-its-the-body-politic/
Durant, Will. *Will Durant Quotes*. 2018. https://www.brainyquote.com/quotes/will_durant_164277

Genetic Study of Andaman Islanders Uncovers New Human Ancestor. Haaretz. 2016
https://www.haaretz.com/archaeology/genetic-study-finds-new-human-ancestor-1.5418525

Viruses That Can Lead to Cancer. Cancer.org. 2018
https://www.cancer.org/cancer/cancer-causes/infectious-agents/infections-that-can-lead-to-cancer/viruses.html

Viruses and Cancer. Cancerquest.org. 2018
https://www.cancerquest.org/index.php/cancer-biology/viruses-and-cancer

www.ingramcontent.com/pod-product-compliance
Lightning Source LLC
Chambersburg PA
CBHW020409080526
44584CB00014B/1252